GETTING TO KNOW YOU

GETTING TO KNOW YOU

how you can solve your "people puzzles"
and increase success in all your
personal and professional relationships

CHRIS CAREY

CREATIVE communication ™ PUBLICATIONS

atlanta, georgia

GETTING TO KNOW YOU

Cover concept and design, illustrations, and typography
by E. Chris Carey

Edited by Kay duPont, CSP, CPDT

Photographs of Chris Carey: Rick Diamond
All other photographs: PhotoDisc

DISCLAIMER: The purpose of this book is to provide insights regarding relationship skills, motivation, and personal improvement. It is not meant to replace professional counseling for emotional or psychological disturbances. Referral to a qualified counselor or therapist is recommended for issues outside the scope of this publication, which is intended only for general use and not as a specific course of treatment.

Published by CreativeCommunication Publications
Post Office Box 725245, Atlanta, Georgia, 31139 U.S.A.

Printed in the United States of America
Prepublication/Review Edition, July 2001
First Edition, October 2002

ISBN 0-9709307-0-4

Table of Contents

Acknowledgments

Thanks to the many individuals who have enriched my life by patiently encouraging me to discover the what, why, and how of my own personal style. I tend to understand how life works through experience. Once you've read this book, you'll understand what these friends have endured to help me.

My wife, Cindy,
and our daughters, Jessica and Danielle.

My business associates,
Chuck Anderson, Terry Ford, and Rick Herceg.

My peer review committee,
Dr. Tony Alessandra, CSP, CPAE; Dr. Robert Alan Black, CSP;
and Dr. Charles F. Boyd.
(*I asked them, "Please don't let me say anything stupid!"*)

My editor,
Kay duPont, CSP, CPDT.

My prereaders,
Kim Anderson, Steve and Julie Dawson,
Roger and Laura Sitcler, Terry and Sandy Thoms,
Hal and Susan Winderweedle.

My mentors,
John Gurley and Mark Mayberry.

Foreword

It pays to be "people smart!" During my career as a speaker and author, I have consistently emphasized that understanding people is necessary to lead them successfully. This is one reason Chris Carey asked me to write this foreword. Another reason, as Chris told me, is that a short paragraph in one of my own early books, *Be A People Person*, impressed him strongly as he began looking for ways to expand his own influence as a leader a decade ago:

☐ *PERSPECTIVE: How do I see myself? How do I see others? How do others see me? Our perspective determines how far our relationship will develop.*

Over the years, Chris has discovered many helpful answers to these questions and, for this reason, I am happy to recommend *Getting to Know You* as a book that will enlarge your perspective and assist you in building relationships that go the distance.

Harry Truman wrote, "When we understand the other fellow's viewpoint, and he understands ours, then we can sit down and work out our differences." Chris Carey's book, *Getting to Know You*, will help you achieve success in your personal and professional relationships by providing a better understanding of both "the other fellow's viewpoint" and your own.

It's a fun read, too. Chris doesn't bore you with dry be-havioral theory, but provides practical examples that will help you solve what he calls the "people puzzles" in life. What he shows you about yourself may surprise you or it may confirm what you've known all along. Either way, you can begin putting it to work in your relationships immedi-ately, in both your family life and your work.

Many people have said they wish they had been taught these life skills in high school or college. Whether you are just starting out on your own, or if you have a lifetime of experience, now is the right time to read this book!

John C. Maxwell, Founder
The INJOY Group
Atlanta, Georgia

Preface

I wrote this book! I love being a writer—not actually the *writing*, but the *being* part. It's a glamorous role that causes people to say, "Ohhh, a writer! I've always wanted to be one...."

The actual *writing* is the not-glamorous-at-all reality that seethes behind the scenes. Winston Churchill understood. He said, "Writing a book is an adventure. To begin with, it is a toy and an amusement. Then it becomes a mistress; then it becomes a master; then it becomes a tyrant. In the last phase, just as you are about to be reconciled to your servitude, you kill the monster, and fling him to the public."

Pulitzer Prize winning sportswriter Red Smith faced the writing monster daily, and he had his own technique. "There's nothing to writing," he claimed. "All you do is sit down at a typewriter and open a vein." So, as long as you understand and appreciate my vein-opening "sacrifices" to bring this book to print, you can get on with the reading.

Actually, I am consoled somewhat by the thought that *you* will have to deal with the monster now. I have flung it, and you have picked it up. Whether you are reading it to gain insights for your personal life or your professional relationships, you'll find that *reading* it requires *you* to "open a vein" too.

In other words, this book will not be a "passive read." Its plan is to draw you in...inspire you to imagine how good your life can become if you put it into practice...provide some practical ways you can demonstrate its value in your own life...motivate you to consider some issues you haven't thought through before...and then cause you to recommend it to your friends!

What this book is about:

I've read that Harvard University, the Carnegie Foundation, and Stanford Research Institute studied career paths and found that 15% of success in finding a job, keeping a job, and moving ahead in a job was related directly to *technical* knowledge and skills, while 85% was related directly to knowledge about and skill with *people.*

So this book is about "people skills." It's about you...and the people you *work* with every day...and the people you *live* with every day. It explains the ups-and-downs you experience in your professional and personal interactions. (It's *not* about psychobabble or catchphrases. Keep reading—you'll like it!)

Why I wrote this book:

I've never known a person who couldn't benefit from improved "people skills." Because I've always made my living in "people businesses," I've had to read many books on relationships, skill-with-people, self-improvement, management, temperament, and more, but somehow the good information in them seldom caught my attention or spoke to me *personally.*

I had resigned myself to living life as an unsolvable puzzle when a friend showed me how the pieces fit together. I found answers that were straightforward, simple enough to understand, and applicable in every aspect of my life.

Honestly, I thought I was well educated and widely read, but I had never picked up on these "life basics" before. I was past 40 when I was introduced to the concepts you are about to read. I wrote this book because the information it contains changed my life.

How I wrote this book:

I wrote it by living it and teaching it. The "instant feedback" of a seminar participant's questions and answers, the demand for clearer examples and explanations, the correction of misconceptions, and the challenge by my audiences to make this a topic for *application* rather than *conversation*—these requirements have made this information as practical for your life as it has been for my own. I "worked out the bugs" with live audiences and then set the result to paper.

When I wrote this book:

I spent 20 successful years as a professional entertainer and motivator before I ever understood the information on the following pages. Through my ignorance, I had managed to get my life's practices and priorities totally misaligned and quit the work I loved.

That's when I began looking for answers that would work consistently in my own life, and I began sharing them with others. Eventually, these discoveries introduced opportunities to create and produce seminar content for other presenters. Gradually, I began speaking and teaching again.

When enough people asked me where they could find this information, I started writing it down.

These days, I speak to groups and coach individuals on how this information can change their lives, and it's easier for them to work through it at their own pace, in a book, than trying to make sense of the hastily scribbled notes they make during my workshops and speeches.

Where I wrote this book:

I work downstairs at home—we call my office "The Dungeon." The kids are upstairs with my wife, where we really try to practice this stuff in our day-to-day lives.

Who I wrote this book for:

You. I don't know which specific puzzle pieces you will put in place as you read it, but I believe you will find missing pieces and discover where they fit.

My family. My speaking and writing keeps a roof over their heads. They thank you for buying my books and recordings.

Me. "To whom much is given, much is required." It's a way of giving back, and I am grateful for the opportunity.

E. Chris Carey
Atlanta, Georgia

SECTION I:
THE BASICS
OF PERSONAL
STYLE

GETTING TO KNOW YOU

Chapter 1: Why Are People Different?

This questions is one of the most important anyone can ask. Unless we understand *why* people are different, *how* they differ doesn't count for much.

People are different because they are *supposed to be.* Sometimes *their* differences frustrate *our* differences, but variants are necessary.

"*Seeing* what everybody else has seen and *thinking* what nobody else has seen." That's how Nobel Prize winner Albert von Szent-Gyorgyi explained his breakthroughs in muscle research and cancer studies. That's how I explain people variations.

If you would prefer a quotation from someone whose name you can pronounce, Mark Twain said, "It were not best that we should all *think* alike; it is *difference of opinion* that makes horse races." Difference of opinion creates variety.

What would the world be like if all of us were the same in our attitudes, preferences, and outlooks? I'm sure it would not be an improvement. No human being is qualified to serve as the model for everyone else. Each of us has admirable areas of strength, but with those strengths come lamentable areas of struggle.

So this book is not about getting people to agree with you. It's about understanding how you see life, how they see life, and how to live better together.

Different by design

You don't have to agree with the way I see the world but, in fairness to you, I'll share my personal view. God made us different because He understands the need for variety—in fact, He delights in it.

Indulge me for a minute, even if you're not a person of faith. I won't hit you over the head with a *Bible* on every page, but what the Good Book has to say about our Divine Design is worth thinking through.

Theodore Roosevelt said, "Every thinking man...when he thinks, realizes that the teachings of the *Bible* are so inter-woven and entwined in our whole civic and social life that it would be literally...impossible for us to figure what the loss would be if those teachings were removed."

Wernher Von Braun, father of the U.S. Space Program, noted, "In this age of space flight, when we use the modern tools of science to advance into new regions of human activity, the *Bible*—this grandiose, stirring history of the gradual revelation and unfolding of moral law—remains in every way an up-to-date book."

Dr. George W. Crane wrote, "I have gleaned more practical psychology and psychiatry from the *Bible* than from all other books."

Whether you approach scripture for inspiration or for cultural understanding, many people attest that Biblical literacy provides benefits beyond theology.

Now, let's spend just a minute on what sacred writings say about our different design:

Israel's King David wrote, "For you created my inmost being; you knit me together in my mother's womb. I praise you because I am fearfully and wonderfully made; your works are wonderful, I know that full well" (Psalm 139:13–14). Saint Paul reasoned, in an analogy of the human body, that our differences contribute to a productive whole in keeping with God's design: "If they [body parts] were all one part, where would the body be? As it is, there are many parts, but one body. The eye cannot say to the hand, 'I don't need you!' And the head cannot say to the feet, 'I don't need you!' On the contrary, those parts of the body that seem to be weaker are indispensable...." (1 Corinthians 12:19–22).

Acceptable differences

Of course, not all differences are positive. According to Robert Frost, "You've got to love what's lovable, and hate what's hateable. It takes brains to see the difference." The problem is that we tend to hate things that are *different* and call them *wrong*. We think the world would be better if everyone was as "normal" as we are.

This attitude caused Jesus to ask, "Why do you look at the speck of sawdust in your brother's eye and pay no attention to the plank in your own eye? How can you say to your brother, 'Brother, let me take the speck out of your eye,' when you yourself fail to see the plank in your own eye? You hypocrite, first take the plank out of your eye, and then you will see clearly to remove the speck from your brother's eye" (Luke 6:41–42).

Great Britain's prime minister Benjamin Disraeli said, "My idea of an agreeable person is a person who agrees with me." That's one way to see differences. Here's another from German Chancellor Konrad Adenauer: "We all live under the same sky, but we don't all have the same horizon."

It's your horizon we're examining in this book. Where you stand determines *what* you see, *how* you see, *when* you see, and *why* you see.

Chapter 2:
How Are People
Different?

About 2500 years ago, a Sicilian named Empodocles founded a school of medicine. He taught that everything was composed of 4 elements: earth, air, fire, and water. He believed these "roots" combined in infinite ways and varieties to create all that exists. He is the father of many of the "4-factor" behavioral models. (Although not a behavioral model, an example of a modern 4-factor model is that all of the colors seen on this book's cover come from a blending of only 4 inks: cyan, magenta, yellow, and black. This does not occur haphazardly, but the inks come together in a specific balance and precise proportions.)

A generation after Empodocles, Hippocrates began observing human behavior. He thought climate and terrain affected people's appearance and behavior. So, *mountain* people were warlike and savage; *meadow* people were timid and emotional; *high country* people were gentle and "unmanly"; *bare soil* people suffered through extremes of weather and therefore became hard, haughty, and self-willed. The idea needed work, but it was the first theory about the effects of environment on behavior.

Further thinking led Hippocrates to the formation of his temperament theory (*sanguine, melancholic, choleric,* and *phlegmatic*), and he associated them with 4 bodily fluids (*blood, black bile, bile,* and *mucous*). Later, in the 2nd Century, Claudius Galenus gathered up all the medical knowledge of his time, thus becoming the authority used by subsequent Greek and Roman medical writers. He wrote about the 4 bodily fluids' effects on behavior and temperament. He also stated that the body is acted upon by warmth, cold, dryness, and moisture.

Modern models of behavior

A major development in understanding human behavior came with the publishing of Dr. Carl Jung's *Psychological Types* in the early 20th Century. He identified *thinking, feeling, sensation,* and *intuition* as the 4 psychological functions. Above these functions, he described 2 divisions of "extroverted" and "introverted."

Seven years later, in 1928, Harvard-educated William Moulton Marston published *The Emotions of Normal People,* in which he described what has become a basis for many 4-factor theories of human behavior. (Dr. Marston was a teaching psychologist at Columbia University and is well known for his 1938 book. *The Lie Detector,* and the polygraph techniques he pioneered. Cartoon enthusiasts knew him under the pen name "Charles Moulton," creator of *Wonder Woman.*)

Robert Alan Black, who has been a valuable member of my review committee and received his doctorate in educational psychology, told me that *The Emotions of Normal People* originally listed 8 factors that influence an individual's behavior (based on Marston's observation of 3000 patients). Ultimately, this led to a 4-factor model adopted by Walter Clarke in his *Activity Vector Analysis*, the first behavioral "assessment" instrument.

In a nutshell, the theory states that, when plotted along 2 axes, an individuals' actions tend to be *Active* or *Passive*, depending on how their environment is understood—either *Antagonistic* or *Favorable*. With the 2 axes at right angles, 4 quadrants are created, describing predictable patterns of behavior:

Perception of En vironment	Response	Behavior
Antagonistic	Active	***Dominance***
Favorable	Active	***Influence***
Favorable	Passive	***Steadiness***
Antagonistic	Passive	***Compliance***

Further, the self-concept we learn and use to meet life's experiences aligns with identifiable factors that influence our behavior.

Ultimately, this theory became known by its initials: *The* **DISC** *Model of Human Behavior.* What is so powerful about **DISC** is that it allows us to apply scientific observation to our behaviors. While other ways of trying to understand why we do what we do tend to be *subjective* and *judgmental*, **DISC** gives us an *objective* and *descriptive* "language" for thinking about our attitudes and actions.

Personal style, plain and simple

I promised we wouldn't fall into psychobabble, so what you have just read is about as complex as we're going to get. The point of all this is that people don't do things *against us*, but *for themselves*. So we tend to view our actions through a lens of personal self-interest. I do the things I do because I see through my own personal style's filter. You may respond differently because you have a different filter.

There are ways to precisely measure the differences in our filters. You may have taken a "personality test" at some point in your life. I avoid calling these instruments tests, because the term implies the possibility of "right" or "wrong" answers. Your own style of behavior is neither right nor wrong. It may produce an appropriate, effective response to your environment in one instance and an inappropriate, ineffective response in another. Understanding our **DISC** issues helps us to be more appropriate and effective as we learn when and how to adapt and adjust to events and people.

Versions of this theory operate under other names. As I've said, Walter Clarke's *Activity Vector Analysis* was the first psychological device to use Marston's theory. Several of his original associates left his company and began refining the format. Today, 50 or more companies use descriptive assessments to examine and identify human behavior. You may recognize some of them:

- *Alessandra, Tony: The Platinum Rule*
- *Black, Robert Alan: M.I.N.D. Design™*
- *Cattell's 16 Personality Factor Questionnaire*

- Keirsey-Bates Temperament Sorter
- Korem Profiling System
- LaHaye's Temperament System
- Merrill-Reid Social Styles
- Minnesota Multiphasic Personality Inventory
- Murphy-Meisgeier Type Indicator
- Myers-Briggs Type Indicator
- Inscape (Performax) Personal Profile
- Personality I.D.
- Personality Insights
- RightPath4 Assessment
- Riso-Hudson Enneagram Type Indicator
- Smalley & Trent Personality Inventory
- Strong Interest Inventory
- Target Training International
- Taylor-Johnson Temperament Analysis

Benefits of simplicity

When I read about behavioral styles in the past, something failed to click. I'm not faulting particular systems or writers—and I'm not suggesting that all of the profiles are of equal merit. I'm just saying I needed something practical and applicable to someone, like myself, who is not inclined to contemplate the cosmos.

Some style explanations were so detailed that I missed their practical application to my situation. Others were so technically oriented that I wished I had stayed awake during psychology classes. Some seemed to complicate what should have been straightforward, while others seemed to oversimplify what should be more deeply explored. The labels for behavior styles confused me too. In one system, I was an Idealist; in another, I was a Networker; in still another, a Champion. I've also been compared to an Otter!

I'm for anything that works for you. I'm not opposed to your using any system that helps you to understand yourself and others. You will understand and appreciate *Ds*, *Is*, *Ss*, and *Cs* when we reach the end of this book, and then you can use another label if you prefer. I just think you'll have an easier time remembering and applying **DISC** than some of the others. It's your choice—*use something!*

So how are people different? We have different filters that influence the way each of us behaves. We're not locked in a box by these preferences but, until we understand them, we have little chance of either accepting or altering their unique characteristics. Our filters influence us to behave in different ways:

Bold, adventurous, and competitive	•	**D**
Animated, inspiring, and motivating	•	**I**
Loyal, faithful, and compassionate	•	**S**
Reserved, disciplined, and controlled	•	**C**

Putting DISC to work

Can you see the benefits in understanding your inner motivations? Using **DISC** enables the following to happen:

- Employers include these insights as part of a "new-hire" screening process while revitalizing and redirecting their companies' existing staff members.

- Employment counselors predict and prevent job-site stress and help supervisors make objective performance evaluations. Behavior statistics are used to benchmark peak performance standards for employees.
- Salespeople improve their relational skills with prospects.
- Behavioral style even affects an individual's safety record in certain industries.
- Volunteer organizations learn how to draw the best from each other while recognizing the special contributions each brings to their team.
- Strategic planners find new ways to eliminate opposition and enlist support from those who will be most affected by change.
- Brokers identify financial opportunities that fit within their investors' risk tolerance and eliminate those that fall outside their clients' comfort zones.
- Students discover interests and career paths in which they can truly flourish, rather than simply labor.
- Teachers find ways to instruct that make learning enjoyable to a variety of students, and develop effective and painless classroom discipline methods.
- Family members learn how to communicate on a more honest and open level, developing greater rapport, trust, and intimacy.

Somewhere in that list is a benefit that appeals to your situation. In your home or at your job, what would you like to do with this information?

- *Resolve conflict?*
- *Build better teams?*
- *Establish credibility?*
- *Improve performance?*
- *Negotiate compromise?*
- *Understand differences?*
- *Create a common vision?*
- *Enhance communication?*
- *Manage more effectively?*
- *Influence others' responses?*
- *Compensate for blind spots?*
- *Enlist support for your ideas?*

All of this—and more—is available to you once you get to know yourself. You start by understanding **DISC**!

Chapter 3:
What Makes
People Different?

you can begin to understand your own personal style by thoughtfully answering these 2 questions:
- What is my *PACE?* • What is my *PRIORITY?*

Recognizing your pace

In seminars and workshops, I ask participants how many would say their *PACE* tends to be fast—they talk fast, walk fast, eat fast, react fast, decide fast? If life had a motor, theirs would be "pedal to the metal" most of the time. I ask them to put up their hands if this describes their *PACE*. How do they raise their hands? *Fast*, of course!

Then I ask how many participants would say their *PACE* tends to be slower—they walk and talk somewhat slowly, they enjoy lingering leisurely over their meals, and they decide and react to life's situations at a slower tempo. I ask them to put up their hands if this describes their *PACE*. How do *they* raise their hands? *S-l-o-w-l-y,* of course!

In the top half of the circle (above), write "speed up."

And in the bottom half of the circle, write "slow down." (Your *preference* for *PACE* corresponds to Jung's factors of *extroversion* [faster pace] and *introversion* [slower pace]. We also term the preferences *outgoing* and *reserved*.)

Recognize your priority

Think of *PACE* as your motor and *PRIORITY* as your steering wheel. "What is your *PRIORITY?*" asks: are you steered more toward *tasks* or toward *people*? Of course, conditions and events may cause you to respond differently at times, but which do you prefer when you can choose?

Task-oriented people are concerned with getting the job done. They tend to be more comfortable when involved in achieving a goal or working on a project.

On the other hand, *people-oriented* individuals are more concerned with relating to others. They tend to be more comfortable when involved in friendships or doing activities with others. Relationships are more important to them than most tasks.

In the left half of the circle (above), write "achievement." And in the right half, write "relationship."

You could say that the focus of *task-oriented* individuals tends to be more "high-tech," while the focus of *people-oriented* individuals tends to be more "high-touch."

How about you? Would you say you are more *task-oriented* ("I like to get things done!") or are you more *people-oriented* ("I am happier when I'm involved with people!")?

Put your answers together

Put your finger on either the top half or the bottom half of the circle *(right)*, indicating whether you see your own *PACE* as *faster* or *slower.* Then move your finger either to the left or right in the circle, indicating whether you see your own *PRIORITY* as *tasks* or *people.*

In these 2 moves, you have indicated something special about yourself. You are primarily:

- Faster-paced *and* task-oriented, *or*
- ✔ Faster-paced *and* people-oriented, *or*
- Slower-paced *and* people-oriented, *or*
- Slower-paced *and* task-oriented.

Say hello to your type!

Your motor and steering wheel—your *PACE* and *PRIORITY*—have brought you to one of the 4 quadrants in the circle.

When we add Marston's *D*, *I*, *S*, and *C* letters to the picture, you will begin to see where your personal style fits.

You may be thinking right now that you are more complex than this, that you have some of all 4 types in your style—and you do! But because we have spent so much of our lives adapting and adjusting to work with others, we may not understand the requirements and comfort level of our own *basic* type. Until we understand those 2 elements, we may not know what our type is.

We'll discuss the blending of your secondary **D**, **I**, **S**, or **C** factors later on—including how to complete a scientifically valid assessment that reveals the full blend of your personal style and the ways you typically adjust and adapt to fit in with others.

For now, our goal for this chapter has been reached. You understand how the issues of *PACE* and *PRIORITY* work together to create 4 distinct types of behavior or personal style.

Congratulations—you know more about yourself and others at this moment than most people understand in a lifetime!

Chapter 4: What Makes a "D" Different?

The "compass" on the circle below shows us that people with a **D** type personal style are *fast-paced* and *task-oriented*. They are the movers and shakers in our culture. According to research published by Target Training International (TTI), this set of behavioral traits is the predominant pattern in about 15% of the population.

Remember, **D** stands for *Dominant* in our **DISC** model. **D** type individuals tend to see the world as an antagonistic or challenging environment that must be *controlled*. This explains why they prefer to move quickly to accomplish their goals. This also explains why they tend not to focus on "people issues" and don't respond to issues at a more deliberative pace. Here are some other descriptive **D** words that identify their behavior:

- Dominating—they like to be in charge, in control.
- Directing—they want to call the shots.
- Determined—they conquer whatever is in their way.

- Demanding—they have the ability to deliver and get the job done.
- Doing—they need to meet challenges and make choices.
- Decisive—they are self-confident and don't look back.

What you see is what they've got

Since the **DISC** language expresses observable behavior, it makes sense that, just by watching **D** types in action, you often can identify their traits.

In their book *DISC: The Universal Language,* authors Bill Bonnstetter, Judy Suiter, and Randy Widrick reported a study in which independent judges selected, from a group, individuals whom they saw as being most like the following adjectives:

- Ambitious
- Forceful
- Decisive
- Direct
- Independent
- Challenging

When the selected individuals responded to a **DISC** style assessment, the judges were over 85% accurate in identifying **D** type people. Equally interesting, the selected individuals also viewed themselves as **D** type people more than 85% of the time.

Of course, incidental observation is not always accurate, because we sometimes mask our *basic* or natural style to fit in with others. When our environment demands a different response, many of us manage to adapt. Our *basic* style is most evident when we are under stress (we tend to drop our veneer) and when we're most relaxed (our responses are unguarded, and we enjoy what we are doing).

The needs of a "D"

*D*s enjoy being in charge! They are "prewired" to *want* to be in control. They *need* to be leaders, and it's often stressful for them to serve another leader—particularly one who does not have strong *D* type traits.

You will not often meet a *D* who exhibits self-doubt. They're not conceited; they're *convinced* that they know the way to go! So, *D*s need continual challenges. Without challenges, they become bored, and bored *D*s will create their own challenges. This often results in unexpected "challenges" for others. *D*s need ambitious goals that match their drive and confidence.

People with a lot of *D* *need* to see themselves as winners. As Vince Lombardi said, "Winning isn't everything—but *wanting* to win is." *D*s will often "up the ante" when a loss threatens, and they will do almost anything to win. *Defeat* and *retreat* are not in their vocabulary. They *need* competition.

Strengths of a "D"

- See the big picture.
- Are independent workers who do not rely on others to provide what is needed.
- Are results-oriented.
- Respond to discouraging news by opposing any obstacles to their success.
- Do not become distracted by small details.
- Adapt quickly to changing circumstances.
- Take authority and solve problems swiftly.
- Get to the point quickly in conversations.
- Challenge any lack of commitment.

- Can set a fast pace for others to follow.
- Evaluate the bottom line.
- Are motivated by opportunities for advancement, profit, and power.
- Are driven by a fierce self-will to do what others find impossible.

Struggles of a "D"

In each type, we will see how *areas of struggle* are actually *strengths* that are out of control. The wonderful strengths of **D**s can work to their disadvantage if those strengths are not used sensitively. Here are some possible limitations for those with **D** type traits:

- Because they see the big picture, they can "live" in their future accomplishments—seeing what can be. But they tend to become bored with the details of getting there. As a result, they risk overdelegating their responsibilities to people who don't share the same vision or leadership style.
- Because they are independent workers, they may fail to report to those who share responsibility, or they may make changes without considering the impact on others.
- Because they are results-oriented, they may overlook the value of things not connected directly to their goal.
- Because they oppose obstacles to their success, they may stubbornly push past protective limits.
- Because they choose not to be not involved in details, they risk overlooking the significant while pursuing the spectacular.

- Because they adapt quickly to change, they may not adequately prepare others to change with them.
- Because they seek authority and solve problems swiftly, they risk being presumptuous and insensitive.
- Because they get to the point quickly, their conversations may be abrupt, blunt, or too demanding.
- Because they challenge lack of commitment, they may intimidate others.
- Because they set a fast pace, they may leave behind others who are necessary to ultimate success.
- Because they evaluate the bottom line, they may neglect the refining touches that assure true quality.
- Because they respond to opportunities for advancement and power, they risk taking advantage of others.
- Because they are strong-willed, they may resist explaining their actions.

All of this means that *D*s enjoy conflict. They hear it in most conversations and see it in most interactions. While it tires many other people, conflict gives energy to people with a lot of *D*. Unless they understand this crucial difference, they may "come on too strong" and offend those whose personal style is to avoid conflict.

The primary emotional response of the *D* type is anger. Generally, they have quick tempers and short fuses. This energy serves them well when focused on high-risk projects, where failure is not an option. Impatient to make a decision and move ahead, they communicate directly—even bluntly—and delegate the details to others.

Chapter 5: What Makes an "I" Different?

The "compass" on the circle below shows us that people with an *I* type personal style are *fast-paced* and *people-oriented*. They are the fun-loving optimists in our culture. According to research published by Target Training International, this set of behavioral traits is the predominant pattern in about 30% of the general population.

Remember, *I* stands for *Influence* in our **DISC** model. *I* type individuals tend to see the world as a favorable or receptive environment that should be embraced. This explains why they usually display high trust in building relationships. This also explains why they tend to focus on "people issues" and respond enthusiastically in social situations. Here are some other *I* words that identify their behavior:

- Inducing—they charm people into agreement.
- Inspiring—they cheerfully look for the bright side.
- Interacting—they have many friends and love talking.
- Imaginative—they can make a difficult task fun.

- Interesting—they have great stories and experiences.
- NO • Impulsive—they make decisions based on feelings.

What you see is what they've got

Just as we saw with the **D** type style, you can identify **I** types by watching them in action. The independent judges mentioned on Page 20 also selected individuals whom they saw as being most like these adjectives:

- Expressive
- Enthusiastic
- Friendly
- Demonstrative
- Talkative
- Stimulating

Again, the judges and the selected individuals agreed over 85% of the time.

I stated this earlier, but it's important to note again that simple observation is not always accurate because we can adapt our natural style to fit in better with others. When our environment demands a different response, many of us manage to adapt. When we are stressed, we tend to drop our adapting and go with what has always worked for us. And when we are most relaxed, our responses are unguarded and we respond more naturally.

The needs of an "I"

Is enjoy social activity! They *want* to be uplifting. They *need* to be recognized, and it's often stressful for them to be ignored or dismissed as unimportant. They are sensitive to others' responses to their *I* type traits.

You will seldom meet *Is* who look discouraged—they may ride a wild emotional roller coaster, but they don't stay down for long! *Is need* variety and avoid routine. They become bored with repetitive tasks, and a bored *I* will *create* ways to have fun. In the process, attention to the task may suffer, but morale will increase, at least temporarily. *Is need* short-term goals to help them stay focused.

People with a lot of *I need* to see themselves as popular and accepted. As Mark Twain said, "I can live for 2 months on a good compliment." At times, their spontaneity and enthusiasm seem limitless. They will do amazing stunts to gain approval. "Stranger" is not a word in their vocabulary. *Is need* people to *watch* and *listen* to them.

Strengths of an "I"

- Are outgoing and friendly.
- Use emotion effectively to enlist others' support.
- Welcome new people and new opportunities.
- Make a memorable first impression.
- Express their feelings openly and genuinely.
- Volunteer readily.
- Respond well to surprises.
- Find humor and a positive outcome in otherwise discouraging situations.
- Come up with imaginative options when facing obstacles.
- Think outside the box and act spontaneously.
- Possess and appreciate verbal skills.
- Start new projects enthusiastically.
- Perform well for recognition and want to include everyone who is on the team.
- Are open-minded and willing to accommodate other points of view.

Struggles of an "I"

The strengths of *Is* can work to their disadvantage if not used sensitively. Again, their areas of *struggle* are actually *strengths* that are out of control. Here are some possible limitations for those with *I* type traits:

- Because they are outgoing and friendly, they tend to trust others too easily and align themselves with people who flatter them or say what they want to hear.
- Because they use emotion effectively to enlist the support of others, they can slip into exaggeration and manipulation without being aware of the change.
- Because they welcome new people and opportunities, they have difficulty prioritizing their duties.
- Because they make a memorable first impression, a "silly" or overly spontaneous impression is not easily erased.
- Because they express their feelings openly and genuinely, others may find them too intense or edgy.
- Because they volunteer readily, they tend to overextend themselves with too many commitments.
- Because they respond well to surprises, they may play unwelcome jokes or pranks on others.
- Because they find humor and a positive outcome in otherwise discouraging situations, people may think they don't understand the seriousness of the occasion.
- Because they come up with imaginative options when facing obstacles, they can be unrealistic.
- Because they think outside the box, their responses may damage their credibility among more linear thinkers.

- Because they possess and value verbal skills, they may try talking themselves out of blame rather than accepting it and moving on.
- Because they start new projects enthusiastically, they may not complete projects before losing interest.
- Because they perform well for recognition, they choose projects and team members indiscriminately.
- Because they are so open-minded and accommodating to other points of view, they are impressionable.

This means *Is* are optimistic most of the time, believing dreams can come true, regardless of existing facts and data. They believe it is impossible to do something "beyond your wildest expectations," unless you already *have* wildest expectations.

Their basic emotional response is trust, and others may take advantage of this trait. They often value verbal persuasion skills over actual performance. Fear of social rejection can motivate their performance. They see the positive in negative situations, and are emotionally resilient, bouncing back after disappointment.

Chapter 6:
What Makes an
"S" Different?

The "compass" on the circle below shows us that people with an **S type** personal style are *slower-paced* and *people-oriented*. They are the supporters and encouragers in our culture. According to TTI research, this set of behavioral traits is the predominant pattern in about 35% of the population—more than any other.

Remember, the **S** stands for *Steadiness* in our **DISC** model. **S** type individuals tend to see the world as a favorable or receptive environment that must be *welcomed*. Their passivity explains why they prefer to serve others rather than lead the way. This also explains why they tend not to embrace change or to respond at a quicker *PACE.* Here are some other descriptive **S** words that describe their behavior:

- Supporting—they prefer to work in the background.
- Steadying—they appear calm and reasonable.
- Stabilizing—they are loyal and predictable.
- Sweet—they are pleasant and polite under stress.

- Specializing—they like doing a few things well.
- Sensitive—they are sympathetic to others' needs.

What you see is what they've got

Marston's **DISC** language explains behaviors we observe, so you can learn to identify **S**s by understanding their traits.

In the study referenced by Bonnstetter, Suiter, and Widrick, the team of independent judges selected individuals whom they saw as being most like the following adjectives:

- Methodical
- Systematic
- Reliable
- Steady
- Relaxed
- Modest

Again, **DISC** style assessments verified that the judges were over 85% accurate in identifying **S** type people through observation, and that these individuals correctly identified themselves as **S** type people more than 85% of the time.

Appearances can be deceiving, because our environment often requires us to adapt our behavior. We tend to see more of the natural style displayed when people are under stress and stop adapting or when they are most relaxed and less guarded in their responses.

The needs of an "S"

Ss enjoy finishing what they start. They are born to be completers. They need freedom from conflict, and it is often stressful for them to be involved in projects that lack closure or to work with those who "flit" from task to task.

Ss seldom act selfishly. They want to affirm and respond generously to others whenever possible. They need a repetitive routine and like to be forewarned of changes. They need to finish one assignment before moving to another one. They *need* a few close friends in whom they can confide over the long term. They *need* to be appreciated. People with a lot of **S** *need* to see themselves as respected an-valued. As William James, world-famous philosopher and author of *The Principles of Psychology*, wrote, "The deepest principle in human nature is the craving to be appreciated." The patience of an **S** is not inexhaustible, but they are re-markably longsuffering. They *need* low risk and stable surroundings.

Strengths of an "S"

- Are dependable, even-paced workers.
- Are team-oriented rather than independent.
- Demonstrate tremendous loyalty and work hard for people and causes they believe in.
- Assist others in areas where they have expertise.
- Have outstanding listening skills, even when interrupted.
- Want to understand expectations and outcomes before they begin.
- Stick with methods that are tried and proven.
- Unite factions by using patience and fairness.
- Empathize with other people's problems.
- Finish projects that others neglect or abandon.
- Nurture lasting relationships.
- Keep secrets and confidences.
- Are quiet and unassuming.
- Give their time, assistance, and resources as demonstrations of friendship.

Struggles of an "S"

Here are some possible limitations for those with **S** type traits:

- Because they are dependable, even-paced workers, boosting their *PACE* is difficult when required.
- Because they are team-oriented rather than independent, they wait for instructions rather than initiating.
- Because they are tremendously loyal, they are the last to "pull the plug" when it is necessary.
- Because they quickly assist others in areas where they have familiarity or expertise, they may overtrain or have difficulty establishing priorities.
- Because they have outstanding listening skills, they may make themselves too available to talkers.
- Because they want to understand expectations and outcomes, they are slow in starting new assignments.
- Because they stick with tried and true methods, they resist procedure changes.
- Because they unite factions by using patience and fairness, they try too hard to please and are stressed when their decisions have a negative impact on others.
- Because they demonstrate empathy for people's problems, they may give false signals of agreement.
- Because they finish projects that others neglect or abandon, they may resent that their other team skills are being overlooked or neglected.
- Because they nurture lasting relationships, they make friends slowly and have room for few.
- Because they keep confidences, they expect high levels

of privacy for themselves and are embarrassed easily.

- Because they are quiet and unassuming, they may not easily express their thoughts, ideas, or resentments.
- Because they give so generously (as demonstrations of friendship), they can become very possessive.

All of this contributes to the **S**'s sensitivity to slights and a sense of resentment if their service goes unacknowledged or unappreciated. They really prefer roles in the background, where they can demonstrate loyalty and achieve stability. They need closure and the chance to finish what they have started, whether it's a relationship or a project.

At the same time, their basic emotional response is to "mask" their true emotions. While they are very emotional *internally,* they seem to handle personal tragedies and victories with equal grace. Serving and helping recharges them, so **S**s feel especially fulfilled and satisfied when turning attention from themselves to others.

Chapter 7:
What Makes a
"C" Different?

The "compass" on the circle below shows us that **C**s are *slower-paced* and *task-oriented*. They are the analysts and philosophers in our culture. This set of behavioral traits is the predominant pattern in less than 25% of the general population.

C stands for **C**ompliant in our **DISC** model. **C** type individuals tend to see the world as an antagonistic or challenging environment that must be *corrected.* They prefer to move carefully in assessing their situation and tend not to focus on variable "people issues" nor respond hurriedly. Other **C** words that describe their behavior are:

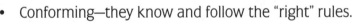

- Conforming—they know and follow the "right" rules.
- Caretaking—they value accuracy and details.
- Calculating—they prefer a balance sheet for decisions.
- Cautious—they "measure twice, cut once."
- Criticizing—their perfectionist nature finds fault.
- Contemplative—they are logical and objective.

What you see is what they've got

Again, you can identify **DISC** behavioral traits just by watching how people act. The independent judges in *DISC: The Universal Language* picked people who demonstrated these traits:

- Analytical
- Exacting
- Contemplative
- Deliberative
- Conservative
- Careful

Again, their accuracy was over 85% in identifying **C** type people whose true style was confirmed through assessment. Likewise, more than 85% of time, these individuals recognized their own preferred behavior as having predominantly **C** traits.

Rather than permitting us to behave as we prefer, our environment often demands that we adapt to fit in. Our *naturally* preferred behavior style is most evident when we are under stress or most relaxed—when we are doing things "our way" to create the results we want.

The needs of a "C"

Cs enjoy knowing the facts! They *want* correctness and precision. They *need* accuracy and order, and it is often stressful for them to be in disorganized surroundings or to work closely with people they perceive as careless or untidy.

Cs are seldom unconcerned; they are protectors of accuracy, tradition, truth—*their* "emotions"! So **C**s need procedures to follow. Without rules, **C**s become unsure and will impose their own perfectionist standards. They prefer established policies and limits rather than problem-solving and corrections. They *need* proof and evidence, which they use to make cautious decisions.

People with a lot of **C** need their environment to be predictable. Patrick Henry observed, "I have but one lamp by which my feet are guided, and that is the lamp of experience." **Cs** do not enjoy working on tasks with unpredictable outcomes. They need reliable facts.

Strengths of a "C"

- Enjoy working by themselves and without interruptions or distractions.
- Conduct thorough research and ask the "tough" questions.
- Are not influenced by trendiness.
- Look for quality and value.
- Are unimpressed by emotional arguments.
- Prefer low-risk methods and safe goals to speculation.
- Respect tradition and hierarchy.
- Are conscientious, maintaining high personal and professional standards.
- Are mindful of small details.
- View problems objectively.
- Use their time and energy efficiently.
- Double-check for accuracy and correctness.
- Look for definition and certainty.
- Pride themselves on their accuracy.

Struggles of a "C"

Here are some possible limitations for those with **C** type traits:

- Because they enjoy working by themselves, they can seem aloof from team relationships.

- Because they conduct thorough research and ask the "tough" questions, they can be viewed as hesitant and suspicious of others.

- Because they are not influenced by trendiness, they may dismiss "hot" topics or fail to recognize or identify with evolving cultural issues.

- Because they look for quality and value, they may not be receptive to bargains or makeshift arrangements caused by a situation's urgency.

- Because they are unimpressed by emotional arguments, they can seem uncaring and detached.

- Because they prefer low-risk methods and safe goals, they are not inspired by others' "dreams."

- Because they respect tradition and hierarchy, they resist innovation and challenges to established order.

- Because they are conscientious, maintaining high personal and professional standards, they prefer associating with people who have the same personal style.

- Because they are mindful of small details, they can become picky perfectionists who are difficult to please.

- Because they view problems objectively, their decisions and loyalties can change based on perception rather than relationship.

- Because they use their time and energy efficiently, they tend to compartmentalize people and tasks.

- Because they double-check for accuracy and correctness, they will not be rushed into giving approval.

- Because they look for definition and certainty, they do not endorse speculative projects.

- Because they pride themselves on their accuracy, they find it very difficult to admit mistakes or to apologize.

These *strengths* and *struggles* contribute to the **C**'s need for consistency and security, which they carefully preserve and protect. They compete with themselves, striving for perfection. Therefore, they tend to be cautious and conventional, rather than being risk-takers.

The basic emotional response of this type is fear. Their aversion to risk and their "by-the-book" approach to events are reliable mechanisms for achieving the security they need. They do not like surprises, and their response to unsettling events is to return to established rules and procedures.

SECTION II: VARIETIES OF PERSONAL STYLE

GETTING TO KNOW YOU

Chapter 8:
DISCover Your Own
Personal Style

U ntil now, we've been laying a basic foundation. Congratulations for staying with it! We're about to see how accurate your self-perceptions are about *TASK* and *PRIORITY.*

The following pages present a simplified personal style survey. It's not as accurate as the multipage, computer-scored, personalized report I use online and in seminars but, it will provide you with some ground-level understanding, so that when we start thinking about *Style Blends* and *Strengths and Struggles,* and *Adapting and Adjusting,* you'll be able to relate to the ideas on a more personal level.

This is not a test. There are no "right" or "wrong" answers. There is no "pass–fail" connected to your responses. You are just providing an indication of your own preferences—what you are *most like* and what you are *least like* among the descriptive word choices provided by the questionnaire.

In group settings, I have seen some people volunteer their word choices for friends to copy, but it doesn't help anyone's understanding when the group goes home with one person's personal style to share among themselves! Answer realistically—as you *really* are—not as you *wish* you could be, or what your friends *think* about you. Just look at the 4 word choices and decide how closely they describe you. It's normal to have some difficulty choosing. Just do your best, and remember to rate all 4 words every time.

Don't spoil this experience for yourself! Stop! Take fifteen minutes now to read the directions *(below)* and indicate your choices on Page 43. Then follow the simple instructions to create a personal style graph on Page 44.

Interpreting your graph

Directions: Read each of the 4 words across on Line 1. Then rate the words on a scale of **4** (the word that is *most like you*) through **1** (the word that is *least like you*).

Use each of the numbers (**4**, **3**, **2**, **1**) only once on every line—as in the example below. Base your selections on how you tend to behave most naturally, regardless of whether you think of it as your "best" behavior.

Remember, this is not a "test." There are no "right" or "wrong" answers. Be yourself!

If you place a piece of carbon paper face down between the word choices (Page 47) and the answer key (Page 49), your choices will be marked automatically on the answer key for easier scoring. Otherwise, you will transfer these selections manually when you are instructed how to do so.

Again, in each line, make sure to rate each set of 4 words, using all 4 numbers only once. As shown in the example, *do not use the same number twice in any line. Instead, make sure every number is used only once per line.*

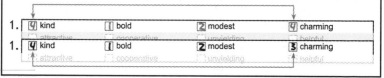

#				
1.	☐ kind	☐ bold	☐ modest	☐ charming
2.	☐ attractive	☐ cooperative	☐ unyielding	☐ helpful
3.	☐ competitive	☐ precise	☐ cheerful	☐ caring
4.	☐ risk-taking	☐ entertaining	☐ trusting	☐ calculating
5.	☐ observant	☐ determined	☐ playful	☐ even-tempered
6.	☐ sociable	☐ steady	☐ independent	☐ solitary
7.	☐ cautious	☐ daring	☐ convincing	☐ satisfied
8.	☐ impulsive	☐ tranquil	☐ dynamic	☐ lenient
9.	☐ outspoken	☐ talkative	☐ restrained	☐ detailed
10.	☐ peaceful	☐ delightful	☐ decisive	☐ warm-hearted
11.	☐ amusing	☐ consenting	☐ calm	☐ assertive
12.	☐ perfectionist	☐ pioneering	☐ optimistic	☐ ready to please
13.	☐ gentle	☐ humble	☐ confronting	☐ lighthearted
14.	☐ in-charge	☐ follows the rules	☐ likes being with others	☐ willing to share
15.	☐ visionary	☐ inspiring	☐ moderate	☐ specific
16.	☐ cooperative	☐ impressionable	☐ exacting	☐ unconquerable

Score Your Responses: *Your responses indicate preferences toward particular characteristics of* **D**, **I**, **S**, *and* **C** *behaviors. When you count the number of responses for each type, you will be able to register them on a graph (below) that shows your most predominant (intense) trait(s) and your supporting traits. It is not unusual to have 2, or even 3, trait-sets score above average.*

How to Score: *If you have used carbon paper between the pages, your number responses appear in the boxes on Page 45. If not, copy the numbers into those boxes now. How many points (numbers) did you score for* **D**? *Write the points value in the gray* **SCORE BOX** *(below left). Then do the same for your* **I**, **S**, *and* **C** *points. If these 4 numbers do not total 160, you have skipped a response. Fix it now, before making your graph.*

How to Create Your Graph: *On the graph below, circle the number in the* **D** *column that matches the* **D** *points in the gray* **SCORE BOX**. *Then, circle each number in your* **I**, **S**, *and* **C** *columns to match those responses. If you do not see your exact number, circle the next lowest number. Then, draw lines to connect the circles, left to right (as shown in graphs on Pages 47–50) to create a line graph of your personal style.*

D I S C

	D	I	S	C
high	64	64	64	64
	60	60	60	60
	54	54	54	54
	50	50	50	50
above average	45	45	45	45
	40	40	40	40
(midline)	36	36	36	36
below average	32	32	32	32
	30	30	30	30
	24	24	24	24
	20	20	20	20
low	16	16	16	16

SCORE BOX

How many **D** points? _____

How many **I** points? _____

How many **S** points? _____

How many **C** points? _____

(NOTE: These must total 160 points!)

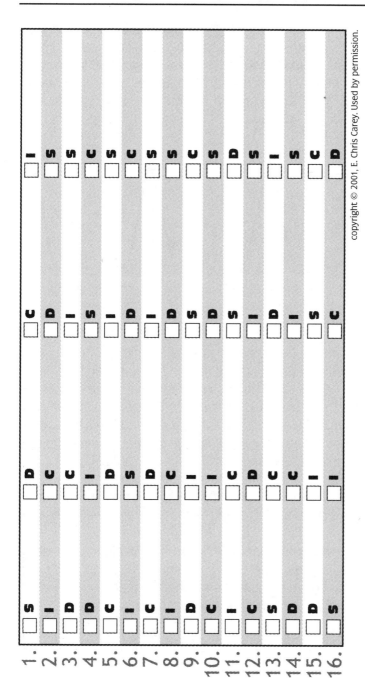

There are many varieties among the 4 basic personal types. For example, you might have only *1* of the 4 types intense enough to be *above the midline* in your personal style, as shown here and described in Chapters Four through Seven. These "pure" styles are not as common as you might sup-

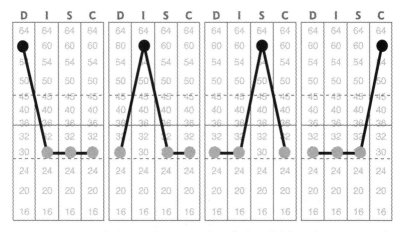

pose. Few people have a personal style in which only one type is so intense that the others have no significant influence.

When people say, "I'm a **D**," they are describing the most observable of their traits and characteristics. The story is almost always deeper than that. For most of us, our personal style is a blend of **D**, **I**, **S**, and **C**, with 2—or even 3—styles being strong enough to rise above the midline. It's very helpful to know your main "driver," but it is modified by subordinate factors that support your most intense traits. This "blend" makes it easier for you to adapt and adjust your style—and to identify with the thoughts and feelings of others.

On the following pages, you can see 6 "blends" for each of the basic types. One type predominates (signified by the black dot), but it is modified by the presence of the other types (signified by the darker gray dots).

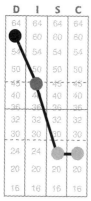

Dominance
Influence

This **D-I** blend is very fast-paced and active. While primarily task-oriented, you can see a need for variety and sociability.

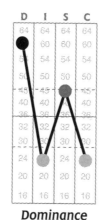

Dominance
Steadiness

This **D-S** blend may seem contradictory because its most intense traits are opposites—*fast/task-oriented* with support from *slower/people-oriented*.

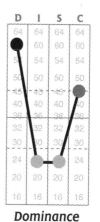

Dominance
Compliance

This **D-C** blend is very focused on *task* accomplishments. The supporting trait of accuracy helps them with details as they work quickly.

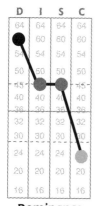

Dominance
Influence
Steadiness

This **D-I-S** blend is *task/fast-paced*, but you see an increased level of people-orientation. Attention to detail is not a natural strength.

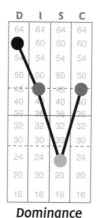

Dominance
Influence
Compliance

This **D-I-C** blend shares some *fast-paced, people* traits along with some *slower-paced, task* traits. Sensitivity to others is not a natural strength.

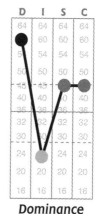

Dominance
Steadiness
Compliance

This **D-S-C** blend prefers *tasks*, but can be diplomatic and supportive. Flexibility in planning and working is not a natural strength.

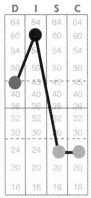

Influence
Dominance

This **I-D** blend is very outgoing and energetic. While *people-oriented*, they are restless without things to do and jump from project to project.

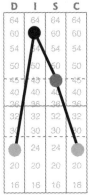

Influence
Steadiness

This **I-S** blend is expressive and emotional. Because they are *people-oriented*, relationships (rather than tasks) are their priority.

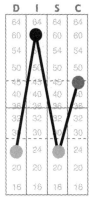

Influence
Compliance

This **I-C** blend may seem contradictory because its most intense traits are opposites—*fast/people-oriented* with support from *slow/task-oriented*.

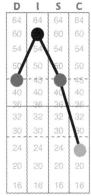

Influence
Dominance
Steadiness

This **I-D-S** blend is high in people skills, but reaching goals and accomplishing tasks is important. Attention to detail is not a natural strength.

Influence
Dominance
Compliance

This **I-D-C** blend inspires confidence using analytical strengths. Therefore, sensitivity to the emotional needs of others is not a natural strength.

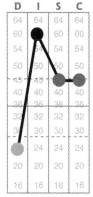

Influence
Steadiness
Compliance

This **I-S-C** blend is strongly *people-oriented* with analysis skills. They are peacekeepers, so acting decisively is not a natural strength.

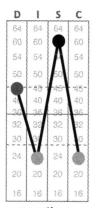

Steadiness
Dominance

This **S-D** blend seems contradictory because its most intense traits are opposites—*slower/people-oriented* with support from *fast/task-oriented* traits.

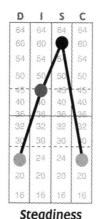

Steadiness
Influence

This **S-I** blend has a warm demeanor and people-centered approach to life. They prefer providing encouragement and support to being an out-front leader.

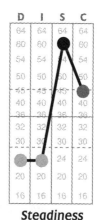

Steadiness
Compliance

This **S-C** blend tends to be very quiet and cautious because of its slower pace. They complete tasks well because they are detail-oriented people-pleasers.

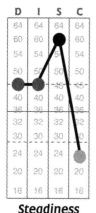

Steadiness
Dominance
Influence

This **S-D-I** blend is people-oriented, with good goal-setting skills. They are practical and "bottom-line." Logical analysis is not a natural strength.

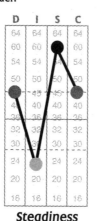

Steadiness
Dominance
Compliance

This **S-D-C** blend is open to people, while being reserved and conscientious. Ability to inspire enthusiasm in others is not a natural strength.

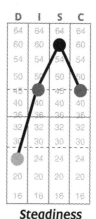

Steadiness
Influence
Compliance

This **S-I-C** blend is *people-oriented*, while being able to work accurately and logically. Proactive decision-making is not a natural strength.

Compliance
Dominance

This **C-D** blend is very *task-oriented*. It is objective and logical, while its secondary traits help it to be effective as a decision-maker.

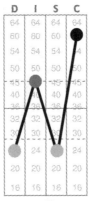

Compliance
Influence

This **C-I** blend may seem contradictory because its most intense traits are opposites—*slower/ task-oriented* with support from *faster/ people-oriented* traits.

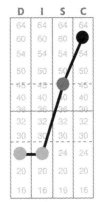

Compliance
Steadiness

This **C-S** blend is focused on accuracy and detailed tasks. Because of its secondary traits, it prefers to specialize in one task at a time.

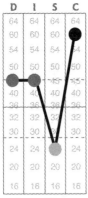

Compliance
Dominance
Influence

This **C-D-I** blend is competent and *task-oriented*, with focused verbal skills. For this blend, warm approachability is not a natural strength.

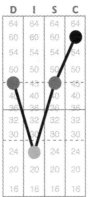

Compliance
Dominance
Steadiness

This **C-D-S** blend excels at problem-solving with logic, achievement, and sensitivity as tools. Personal transparency is not a natural strength.

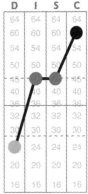

Compliance
Influence
Steadiness

This **C-I-S** blend tends to make a cautious, sensitive, and agreeable team worker. Taking initiative is not a natural strength.

Chapter 9:
How Blends
Define Personal Style

Even if your **D** type traits are most intense, you know there is more than **D** at play in your personal style, don't you? You probably also recognize some **I**, **S**, and **C** traits, as shown in your graph.

Marston also recognized this truth. He acknowledged that all people exhibit all 4 behavioral factors in varying degrees of intensity. In fact, the *intensity*, or strength, of these factors is a key in your style.

The blend of **D**, **I**, **S**, and **C** traits in your personal style has given you a natural ability to adapt and adjust more readily to some circumstances than to others. We alluded to this near the end of the last chapter.

We have described mostly "pure" traits of **D**, **I**, **S**, and **C** until now, depicting how an individual would behave if we could isolate these most intense traits from the influence of the others—if that's all you had to work with and operated without making appropriate adjustments.

If you have inquisitive **C** traits, you'll be glad to know there are *Target Training* statistics showing how few people have only *one* above-average set of traits with which to work:

Style Traits	Pace/Priority	Population
Purely **D**	fast-paced/task-oriented	12 per 1,000
Purely **I**	fast-paced/people-oriented	10 per 1,000
Purely **S**	slower-paced/people-oriented	9 per 1,000
Purely **C**	slower-paced/task-oriented	3 per 1,000

How "blends" work

If these statistics reveal nothing else, they show that 966 out of 1,000 people are significantly influenced by more than one set of traits. This means we may adapt to some situations better than others because we have *some* familiarity and experience with characteristics that enable and support us when we *must* adjust.

Looking at the 4-quadrant circle diagram we have used to explain PACE and PRIORITY, you can see that certain qualities in each type complement different halves of the circle. For instance:

The top half of the circle represents the **D** and **I** styles. Both are *fast-paced—extroverted* and *active*. This means they are *outgoing* and more willing to *advance* when opposed.

The bottom half of the circle represents the **S** and **C** styles, both of which are *slower-paced—introverted* and *passive*. This means they are *reserved* and more willing to *pull back* when opposed.

Those who have styles in the right half of the circle tend to see their environment as favorable rather than antagonistic. Their common bond is not found in their *PACE*, but in their *people PRIORITY*. Their strength is in relationship-building more than critical thinking. Teamwork, inclusion, consensus, and communication are their best tools.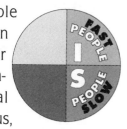

The left half of the circle represents both the **D** and **C** styles. These do not have *PACE* in common, but they share the *PRIORITY* of *task*. They also share a view that their environment is more antagonistic. The **D** *challenges* the environment to *control* it, and the **C** *defends* against it to *correct* it. Both styles use planning, logic, strategy, and evaluation against their antagonistic surroundings to a greater degree than those who operate from the right half of the circle.

Look at this diagram *(right),* and you will recognize commonalities for your own most intense type within its closest neighbors. Even if they are not strong enough to be above the midline, you've got some *PACE* characteristics in common with one neighbor

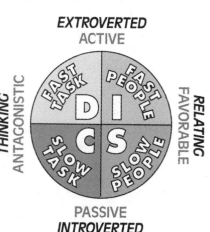

EXTROVERTED
ACTIVE

THINKING
ANTAGONISTIC

RELATING
FAVORABLE

PASSIVE
INTROVERTED

and some *PRIORITY* characteristics in common with the other:
- **D** shares *fast PACE* similarities with **I** and *task PRIORITY* similarities with **C**.
- **I** shares *fast PACE* similarities with **D** and *people PRIORITY* similarities with **S**.
- **S** shares *people PRIORITY* similarities with **I** and *slower PACE* similarities with **C**.
- **C** shares *task PRIORITY* similarities with **D** and *slower PACE* similarities with **S**.

Notice that we don't see similar characteristics between your most intense style's traits and its opposite in the circle:

D shares no *PACE* or *PRIORITY* similarities with **S**.

I shares no *PACE* or *PRIORITY* similarities with **C**.

S shares no *PACE* or *PRIORITY* similarities with **D**.

C shares no *PACE* or *PRIORITY* similarities with **I**.

This is why most people have the greatest struggle understanding the behavior of those who have *opposite* styles. They don't have the *filters* or the *feelings* of their opposite type. As a result:

- **D** types often are puzzled by **S** types and think they are too timid and shy.
- **S** types often are puzzled by **D** types and think they are too pushy and boastful.
- **I** types often are puzzled by **C** types and think they are too particular and analytical.
- **C** types often are puzzled by **I** types and think they are too reckless and impulsive.

Unless we understand why and how the differences work together, how can we understand each other?

No ideal style

There is no "perfect" or ideal style. Each has the potential to make significant contributions in any project or relationship using the *strengths* of that style's traits or characteristics. Each has the potential to derail projects and relationships by becoming unbalanced in using those same *strengths*.

We described a few limitations when we looked at the "blend" graphs (Pages 47–50). The descriptions attempted to demonstrate that every style has issues to deal with and contributions to make. Once you understand the 4 types, it becomes easy to understand how blends behave.

Dr. Charles F. Boyd has written a wonderful book on **DISC** and children, *Different Children, Different Needs* (Sisters, OR: Multnomah Publishers, 1994). He is also an expert at reading graphs and teaching others how to interpret them. I credit Charlie with my own skills in this area and, as several of my clients have commented, once you understand how to read the graphs, the styles are self-evident. This is because the graphs potentially reveal our strengths, our areas of struggle, and the areas where we lack understanding or experience.

For instance, draw your Page 44 graph again, using the blank form on the next page, and we'll have a quick graph-reading lesson.

First, circle the letter at the top of the graph that represents your most intense type. This is the most predominant type in your style, having the highest number and the highest plotting point on your graph.

Your least intense type has the lowest number and plotting point on your graph. If you look at the chapter describing its traits, you will probably admit that it is the type you understand least. These are the traits of which your natural style has the least.

Between these 2 high and low plotting points are the plotting points of the other 2 types that make up your own *DISC* profile. If

D	**I**	**S**	**C**
high	64	64	64	64
	60	60	60	60
	54	54	54	54
	50	50	50	50
above average	45	45	45	45
	40	40	40	40
(midline)	36	36	36	36
	32	32	32	32
below average	30	30	30	30
	24	24	24	24
	20	20	20	20
low	16	16	16	16

either (or both) of these 2 points is above the midline, it plays a significant role in supporting and modifying your highest scoring type. This supporting style offers a set of tools that makes you more naturally relatable and adaptable than a "pure" style would be. Because this style is close at hand, you may "borrow" from it to suit your purposes.

The "higher" the plotting point, the greater its *D, I, S,* or *C* impact on your own natural behavior. You have "stronger," more intense traits of this type when your plotting point is higher. Likewise, the "lower" your plotting point, the "weaker" this type is in your personal style—so you have less intense traits of this type when your plotting point is lower.

Chapter 10:
Style Strengths and Struggles

This is a good spot to discuss a concept I identify as *strengths and struggles*. Most who write or teach about **DISC** refer to these as "strengths and *weaknesses*." I think the latter term preconditions us for failure, so I don't use it. A "weakness" can be viewed as a *handicap* or a *disability*. To be handicapped suggests that what you have is not enough to be effective. When you learn to use your personal style's traits and characteristics appropriately, you can become very effective. Likewise, to be "disabled" suggests that you are incapable of doing something. Seeing yourself as incapable does nothing to encourage your personal growth.

However, if you learn to say, "This is an area of *struggle* for me...," you acknowledge both your *capacity,* as well as your *need,* to do something about it. You acknowledge your ability and responsibility to grow and improve in important areas in your life.

When you see that you have areas of *strength* because of your particular style, you can identify them. However, when you see that you are using those *strengths* indiscriminately, inappropriately, or excessively—so they become a disadvantage—you can say, "This is an area of *struggle* for me...."

Also, when you recognize a need for skills that are not natural for your style, you can say, "These are *struggle* areas for me...." Then, in any area where you acknowledge a need for improvement, you are not saying, "I am handicapped, incapable, and defective." You are saying, instead, "I will admit to having this limitation, but I'm going to work at improving it." That's what this book is about.

The barrel theory

A theory is promoted by many self-improvement teachers that, in creating a more positive self-image, you should concentrate on your strengths and ignore your "weaknesses." I believe that, when you ignore weaknesses, they will *remain* weaknesses in every sense, rather than *becoming* struggles you can overcome.

An opposing theory declares that we can become more effective by improving in our struggle areas rather than by polishing up the areas where we already shine.

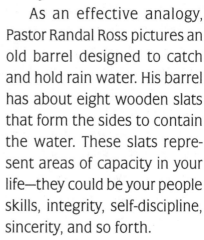

As an effective analogy, Pastor Randal Ross pictures an old barrel designed to catch and hold rain water. His barrel has about eight wooden slats that form the sides to contain the water. These slats represent areas of capacity in your life—they could be your people skills, integrity, self-discipline, sincerity, and so forth.

However, one slat is not as tall as the others. Randal points out that the barrel's capacity is no greater than the height of the shortest slat. Anything added above this limit leaks out! He reasons that your *affective* capacity is limited by the deficiencies you permit to drain your life. I believe this is true of the *strengths* and *struggles* of your personal style.

There is more involved in determining your capacity than only the *strengths* of your style. The *struggles* that drain your effectiveness will continue to do so until they are addressed. At the very least, you should be aware of your style's "leak" and location so you know what reserves you can count on when you need to draw from them—and which you can't.

There is an even greater lesson to be learned from Randal Ross's barrel: just a small improvement in the defective slat increases the capacity of the entire barrel, because every slat is able to retain more when you improve the weak one! A small, focused improvement causes significant improvement overall.

What does your barrel hold?

Your personal style has equipped you to be effective in many areas of life—for some purposes more than others. Maybe your barrel's purpose isn't to hold water at all. Maybe it's designed to holds nails...or crackers!

For example, if you are primarily *task-oriented* and *slower paced* (possessing a lot of **C** type traits), you will probably be more effective and content working in a job that requires your *strengths* of accuracy and critical thinking, rather than a job that demands you *struggle* with hospitality and flexibility in dealing with people (a better fit for someone with a lot of *I* traits).

At the same time, understand that being able to work *only* on *C* type projects limits you needlessly. The quality of your life and work will improve as you build some strong "people skills" into your repertoire. Likewise, if you have a lot of *I* type traits, the quality of your life and work will improve as you add analytical and detail skills to your capabilities. Such improvements do not come easily or naturally (that's why we call them *struggles*), but they are very worthwhile.

Improving a deficiency results in overall improvement—just as fixing the deficient slat improves the capacity for service in the whole barrel!

Here's an odd thought: why would someone want a *rain* barrel to be watertight? So the water wouldn't leak out, of course! But wouldn't you also want a *cracker* barrel to be watertight so water wouldn't leak in? This would be a good idea for a keg filled with nails too, given their inclination to rust when around moisture.

What does this question have to do with your style? You may not identify a particular trait or characteristic as being important to the work you are doing now, but your "barrel" always has potential usefulness. If you make yourself as serviceable and versatile as possible, you will increase the available options in your life.

"Characteristics" are not "character"

It is important to understand that an individual's personal style is not an indicator of morals or values. **DISC** is a system for identifying a person's preferred style by observing his or her behavior. *Values* are not readily observable, but they are discovered by exploring thoughts and discussing attitudes.

Is a hammer "good" when it builds a church and "bad" when it hits someone on the head? No, it's a "neutral" tool; only the way in which it's *used* can be good or bad. It's the same with styles. How you *use* your type's characteristics can be moral or immoral, but the characteristics themselves are neutral.

So it's a mistake to look at someone who has a lot of **D** characteristics and assume, "She is pushy and doesn't care what happens as long as she wins!" Or to say of someone with lots of **I**, "He has to be a goofball—all talk and jokes with nothing to back it up!" Or to say of a person who shows lots of **S** traits, "He's so shy he couldn't even lead a group in silent prayer. He can't take charge!" Or to say of someone with many **C** features, "She is a cold fish, obviously too proud to accept our help!"

Stereotypes and misunderstandings are precisely why you need to be cautious when looking at each type's *strengths* and *struggles*. We too easily translate *struggles* into *faults*. When we understand this error, we can head off conflicts and set each other up for greater success.

A popular Broadway play is called *I Love You, You're Perfect—Now Change!* Such attitudes are the result of seeing *faults*, rather than understanding *differences*. If you want to avoid becoming embattled and embittered in relationships, a key is "**DISC**overing" the *why* behind those differences.

Armed with this understanding, a mature person will be able to move from *annihilating* another's differences to *tolerating* those differences. That's progress! If we gain real competence in working with style differences, we'll progress all the way to *celebrating* the differences that *complete* what we lack.

Here's a good starting place: consider others' *natural strengths* that are not well-developed in you. How can your life or work improve by using those strengths? Then look at how you can use your *natural strengths* to enhance people who lack what you have. Do this rather than try to "fix" others to be more like yourself. Draw upon their complementary *strengths.*

How do you respond when someone treats you as a "project" to be fixed? How do you receive their lack of tolerance, looks of exasperation, condescending tone, icy detachment, sarcastic comments? Not well at all!

Regardless of style, no one responds positively to a hostile environment! You will get far more cooperation and progress by working with people's *strengths* than by trying to fix what you perceive as their weaknesses. Here's a clue: while *tolerating* people's differences is better than *annihilating* them, we all prefer to go where we are *celebrated,* not just *tolerated!* Celebrate people and their uniqueness.

Also, learn how to be as gracious with yourself as I am asking you to be with others. First, fairly and honestly identify your own style's excellent *strengths.* Then recognize your *struggles* and the *benefits* to be found in your own personal growth. Remember the rain barrel—but don't see yours only as "half-empty"!

Typical strengths and struggles for Ds	
How we see ourselves	How others may see us
• Bold	Arrogant •
• Competitive	Combative •
• Risk-Taking	Reckless •
• Determined	Headstrong •
• Independent	Autonomous •
• Outspoken	Tactless •
• Decisive	Dictatorial •
• Assertive	Pushy •
• Pioneering	Predatory •
• Confronting	Offensive •
• Strategic	Ruthless •
• Direct	Rude •
• Self-Confident	Disrespectful •
• Self-Assured	Conceited •
• Challenging	Intimidating •
• Authoritative	Dogmatic •
• Daring	Defiant •
• Ambitious	Impatient •
• Persistent	Demanding •
• Goal-Oriented	Obsessive •

Typical strengths and struggles for Is

How we see ourselves	How others may see us
• Trusting	Indiscriminate •
• Optimistic	Unrealistic •
• Charming	Manipulative •
• Amusing	Frivolous •
• Sociable	Fickle •
• Convincing	Exaggerating •
• Spontaneous	Impulsive •
• Enthusiastic	Gushy •
• Relational	Situational •
• Communicative	Gossipy •
• Lighthearted	Shallow •
• Flexible	Unfocused •
• Articulate	Effusive •
• Passionate	Illogical •
• Talkative	Self-Promoting •
• Imaginative	Distractible •
• Energetic	Frenetic •
• Gregarious	Loud •
• Persuasive	Fast-Talking •
• Ingenious	Impractical •

Typical strengths and struggles for Ss

How we see ourselves	How others may see us
• Even-Tempered	Complacent •
• Stable	Unemotional •
• Helpful	Patsy •
• Steady	Dispassionate •
• Satisfied	Hesitant •
• Peaceful	Timid •
• Team-Oriented	Dependent •
• Cooperative	Spineless •
• Good Listener	Closemouthed •
• Methodical	Slow •
• Patient	Passive •
• Predictable	Monotonous •
• Supportive	Enabling •
• Empathetic	Self-Inflicting •
• Loyal	Possessive •
• Nonconfronting	Dishonest •
• Sensitive	Fragile •
• Traditional	Resistant •
• Neutral	Uninvolved •
• Forgiving	Grudging •

Typical strengths and struggles for Cs

How we see ourselves	How others may see us
• Modest	Severe •
• Precise	Picky •
• Calculating	Scheming •
• Observant	Nosy •
• Solitary	Unsociable •
• Cautious	Distrustful •
• Detailed	Fixated •
• Exacting	Perfectionist •
• Accurate	Faultfinding •
• Compliant	Rigid •
• Efficient	Uncaring •
• Orderly	Compulsive •
• Logical	Emotionless •
• Conscientious	Fretful •
• Consistent	Stubborn •
• Idealistic	Theoretical •
• Analytical	Suspicious •
• Questioning	Prying •
• Private	Evasive •
• Excellent	Superior •

A shoe that fits

If you're at all like me, you found something in these lists personally offensive—*how could anyone think that of me?* This is an important question to ask yourself as you check the lists again. (For inclusion in your planner or organizer, the Strengths and Struggles Charts and other graphics from this book can be downloaded from *www.ChrisCarey.com*.)

Your lists of "How we see ourselves" and "How others may see us" are *possibilities,* not *predictions.* How they apply to you is influenced by the intensity of the other 3 types in your personal style. Your *blend* of *D, I, S,* and *C* makes a difference. So, as you cross out a potential *struggle* in one list, you may have to put a check mark by another in a different list.

When you looked at the list of *strengths* (how we see ourselves), you probably didn't find anything objectionable in any of the 4 types. Honestly, I wish all the *strengths* of every type were mine. In one way or another, I hope to acquire them one day. For now, progress comes as I acknowledge some *struggles* in my style (how others may see me) and identify my need for some of the *strengths* I see in others.

Lists like these are helpful because they help us see what others may perceive about us at times.

Here's a practical, real-life example. I was trying to explain to my wife why I was not to blame for a problem. (I don't remember whether it was something I had done wrong or something I had failed to do altogether. What I do remember is that I presented a "believable" explanation for everything she brought up. I was blameless, if she could simply understand the situation!)

This occurred before we understood anything about **DISC**, but it would be fair to say my every *I* trait was working overtime for me as I presented my defense—and every one of Cindy's **C** traits was conscientiously dissecting my arguments. She was totally unconvinced. The end of our "discussion" arrived when she said to me, "You are the most manipulative human being I have ever met!"

Of course, I was offended—*misunderstood* and offended. How could she think such a thing, let alone say it out loud? Then I realized it was probably hormones and anger! Certainly no one in a logical state of mind would misjudge me in this way.

Shortly after this, we began to learn about **DISC** and the ways we are wired. We completed the same behavioral assessment I administer to clients today. I was so surprised when I found out that I was not a *logical thinker* but an *emotional relater!* As I read through the computer report created from my word choices, I was amazed to "**DISC**over" the complex patterns of my individual style. Suddenly, I saw a word: *manipulative.* The report said I had the *capacity* to be manipulative.

I thought about it for a while. "Capacity" meant I *could* be...even though I never thought I had been. Then I thought to myself, "Computers don't have hormones, and I haven't done anything to make Microsoft Windows angry with me." I understood that I was dealing with an objective interpretation of my responses, and it said I had the capacity to be a manipulator. Of what—people, situations, events, the truth? It was a sobering moment.

Then I thought, "Well, if I ever have manipulated, I'm sure it was just for everyone's good!"

I'll admit now that this was a poor response to the truth, but a door was opening to a darkened area of my understanding. It was a beginning.

I began to recognize times when I was manipulating people and situations with my quick wit, glib speech, easy charm, and persuasive appeals. I began to see a pattern in my whole life, unchallenged until then.

Perception is everything

Perhaps some of the *struggle* areas listed for your style are not really challenges in your life. If so, feel free to cross them off your list of concerns. But first, think about how others see you. We agreed earlier that *traits* are not the same as *values*, and that *characteristics* are not the same as *character*. However, we judge most people by what we observe in their actions, and this is how most people judge us. So how people *perceive* us determines much of their response to us.

If they *perceive* that I am exaggerating, while I am trying only to *convince* them, then I have a huge obstacle to surmount.

If I am conversing with someone and I try relating to everything they say by telling them all about my similar experiences, they will *perceive* that I am self-centered and self-promoting—even while I am thinking how well I am identifying with them!

Sometimes, the only way we can understand these perceptions is to be exposed to someone who is like us to a higher extreme. When we see how oblivious *they* are to *their* faults, it can cause *us* to reconsider *our* behaviors.

People with a lot of *I* traits take acceptance or rejection very seriously. We draw self-esteem from our perception of how others accept us. So, in the past, when someone called me to task, I usually found a way to "make a funny" in the situation. This was my way of saying, "But you still like me, don't you? You're not *rejecting* me—just *correcting* me, right?" But it didn't often come out that way. Most **D**s and **C**s perceived that I was trying to charm my way out of responsibility and accountability for my actions, and that I didn't take them or my situation seriously. Their response was to land on me even harder because I didn't get it. Quite to the contrary, I *did* get it. In fact, I was dying inside, and this was my coping mechanism—but it only made matters worse.

As I grow in understanding myself and others, I try not to "make a funny" anymore. I know my correctors want me to raise my hand and acknowledge the foul so we can get on with the game. They *are* correcting, not rejecting, me—unless I become defensive and manipulative.

To quote Popeye, "I yam whut I yam!" It would be unreasonable for you and me to try to change everything about ourselves, especially since I believe we are wired as we are by Divine Design.

However, it is totally reasonable for us to *adapt* and *adjust* our styles so we can establish credibility and win the acceptance of others. I know that, when I am dealing with **C** types, about the time I feel I should be checking my pulse, they are thinking that I am thoughtful and amusing! When I adapt well, they look forward to seeing me again. When I adapt poorly, they look forward to going home and locking their doors!

As an *I*, I have learned to adjust so I can increase credibility with those who are more *reserved* or *task-oriented* than I am. Credibility and influence are big things for *Is*. We are wired to seek acceptance, but the approach we take is often detrimental to meeting our need.

Is the same true of your style? What is it you most need and want? How does the perception of others help or hinder you in attaining what you want?

- Do you have predominantly *D* type traits and want control, while others fear what will happen to them if you gain power?
- Do you have predominantly *S* type traits and long for relationships, while others think you are satisfied and self-contained in your life?
- Do you have predominantly *C* type traits and want to be valued for your contributions, while others think you criticize theirs?

As you continue reading, I'll continue to provide examples from my life, hoping you can use them to work through your own personal style issues in a practical way. Understanding this information means you can apply it in your everyday relationships. Knowing the *strengths* and *struggles* of your style offers the gift poet Robert Burns wrote about:

O would some Power the gift give us
To see ourselves as others see us!

SECTION III: IMPLICATIONS OF PERSONAL STYLE

Chapter 11: The Morality in Style

We have established firmly that **DISC** is not a measure of morality, but of observable behavior. It does not consider experience, training, skills, values, education, or intelligence. However, there is a moral component in the ways we choose to express our traits—the way we behave.

You may not have recognized a moral responsibility until now, but you have an obligation to improve your behavior once you begin to understand its impact on yourself and others.

In the *Bible's* book of Romans, Saint Paul says that until he knew God's Law, he was "innocent" of breaking it. But once he understood, he was obligated to it. He understood that he was a sinner. (The Greek word used in the *Bible* for "sin" is *harmatia*. Taken from archery, its original meaning was "missing the target.")

Likewise, you may not have seen a target for your behavior until now. Once you understand how your personal style's *struggles* fall short of the mark, you become more aware of missing the bull's-eye!

Theologically speaking, does lack of understanding God's Law relieve the penalties of missing the target? No, and every day we see how people suffer because of human imperfections. There are consequences, even when we innocently miss the mark. Likewise, whenever our style deficiencies miss the mark, consequences are invoked on others, as well as on ourselves.

As an example, my family suffered greatly when I entered into an ill-considered business partnership. I knew nothing about my personal style and did not understand the style of the new partner I brought into my established business as senior vice president.

He thrived on conflict and confrontation. Those things drained me, so I avoided disagreement. Further, I deferred to him in business decisions because he was *task-oriented*. I was eager to release that responsibility so I could enjoy the *people-oriented* aspects. Beyond wanting harmony, my I style also sought his approval and acceptance, so I was vulnerable to criticism and rejection when he didn't get his way.

It was a recipe for disaster. He took charge, made decisions, and issued decrees without consulting me. In his zeal for control, he undermined my character and credibility through critical comments to others. Three months later, when I pulled my head from the sand, I discovered frustrated employees, angry clients, and debts of more than $150,000.

Did I plan for negative results? No, but "innocence" did not relieve me of either responsibility or consequences. I never regained the trust of some employees. I spent 2 years apologizing to clients and suppliers, and several more years paying off those bills. To this day, what I regret most is the toll on my family. My wife and kids lost because I didn't understand myself, my needs, my actions, my motivations, or my patterns.

Some of us are more sensitive than others, so I want to make it clear that I am not trying to make anyone feel guilty over past failures. I just want the consequences of our unadjusted behaviors to sting enough that we will sense our need to fix whatever isn't working as well as it could. First be aware, then beware!

Finding the target

What is the target for your personal style and behavior? Simply this: to be appropriate in your actions and responses. Whenever what we do is inappropriate, we have missed the target.

The challenge we face is that, in the urgency of the moment, we seldom recognize when we are behaving inappropriately. Whatever we are doing seems rational to us. We believe we are doing what the situation requires or excuses, but we may actually be doing what meets our own needs for the moment, and this is a very different standard. This is a key to understanding our *struggles.*

Our target is acting and reacting in an appropriate manner, so we achieve our worthy goals in ways that honor and affirm the needs of others.

Obstacles to success

Of course, we all have areas where we are lacking in strength. For example, I am not *naturally* detail-oriented; I'm a "big-picture" guy. Because I am now aware of this deficiency, I try to compensate by giving extra attention to details that I previously tended to overlook, and I have learned to use others as backup for this tendency.

However, the greatest damage I have inflicted on myself and others has not been because of my style's deficiencies. My greatest obstacles have come from failing to control the excesses of my *strengths*. Out of balance, my *strengths* lose their potential to bring me to victory!

Consider what happened in my failed business partnership because I ignored the "dark side" of the following traits:

- I am *naturally* a negotiator and a peacemaker.
- I am *naturally* a people-pleaser who performs well for the approval and recognition of others.
- I *naturally* enjoy being with others and prefer "facetime" to task completion.
- I am *naturally* optimistic and enthusiastic about new undertakings.
- I *naturally* look for success in a team effort.
- I *naturally* seek to solve problems by talking about them and seeking agreement with my point of view.
- I am *naturally* open-minded and receptive to the ideas of others.
- I tend *naturally* to open my heart and operate without a hidden agenda.

When all these traits are in balance, they are assets for me. Out of control, they created the following problems:

- Because I am a negotiator, I believed I could appease the problem with my verbal skills. By talking about it, I thought I would somehow be able to resolve it.

- Because I am a people-pleaser, I thought I would be recognized as a "good guy" and dealt with on that "reasonable" basis.

- Because I am better with people than projects, I reasoned that I could successfully delegate bottom-line responsibility to someone else—giving me time to do what I *naturally* preferred.

- Because I am optimistic, I was happily unrealistic about assessing our different views of the business.

- Because I am enthusiastic, I did not guard my expectations for success and ignored warning signs about our "team."

- Because I feel better whenever I talk about problems, I assumed our issues had been resolved after discussing them.

- Because I don't like conflict or rejection, I didn't set limits on his power, and I abdicated my own authority.

- Because I wanted to "look good," I would not admit failings that altered my "good" image, and did not seek objective counsel that might have protected me.

- Because I "needed" to keep up pretenses, I abdicated responsibility to someone who could do the job for me.

- Because I heard what I wanted to hear from my partner at the start, I granted him too much trust far too soon.

- Because I wanted to play, I found it easy to avoid asking difficult questions or demanding explanations.

- Because I felt inadequate to handle finances and business details, I let someone else determine what would be done with my resources and commitments.
- Because I wanted to be liked, I let someone else make and enforce standards and policies.

I failed to recognize basic facts about myself, so I dug a deeper and deeper hole. Should my partner have been answerable for this failure too? Of course, but assigning him blame for taking advantage of my flaws doesn't begin to explain it. Between pride, denial, and ignorance, I made a mess of things.

I came away from the experience knowing I never wanted another one like it, but I still had no grasp of the issues that led me into it. I didn't know how many of these problems could have been anticipated and avoided by understanding key factors in my partner's and my own behavior styles. I was ignorant of my obstacles, but I still had to pay the price. It's not what I didn't know that hurt me as much as what I *thought* I knew. I thought it would all work out *naturally*.

A reasonable response

In his book, *Get Ahead: Scovil's 7 Rules for Success in Management* (Atlanta, GA: Longstreet Press, 2000), Roger Scovil, says the first rule is "Don't make enemies." He writes, "You'll have to be a lot smarter to succeed if you have to do it while being surrounded by people who are eager to see you fall on your face."

We can avoid making enemies by choosing a reason-

D = Dominate

able response every time rather than having a *natural* reaction.

The adult daughter of a man I know has very intense **D** traits. He told her a comment had been hurtful to him, and her reaction was, "Grow up, Dad!" It would have cost her nothing to say, "Dad, I didn't mean to hurt your feelings, and I'm sorry it sounded that way. What I mean is...." It was easier for her to throw blame back on her father than to rein in her aggressiveness. Her *good* tendency to be direct gave way to her *bad* tendency to be blunt. Rather than opening up dialogue, she cut off communication.

As the saying goes, "You pick your friends, but you're stuck with your relatives." The daughter's reaction was forgiven by her father, but the tie between friends or business associates is not as sturdy. Sharp-tongued comments have ended both relationships and careers.

This is why the *Bible* tells us, "A gentle answer turns away wrath, but a harsh word stirs up anger" *(Proverbs 15:1)*. And in Proverbs 25:11–12, Solomon wrote, "A word aptly spoken is like apples of gold in settings of silver. Like an earring of gold or an ornament of fine gold is a wise man's rebuke to a listening ear." An appropriate, reasonable response to life's challenges is a sure way to build respect and acceptance with others. It's the quickest path to getting the results you want.

Frankly, we make enemies through our unguarded, style-based reactions more often than we recognize. Our *strengths* become *weaknesses* when we fail to discipline their use. When we address their vulnerability to being misused, we transform them from *weaknesses* into *struggles* we can overcome.

Ask yourself: *What moral right do I have to continue on a path that causes harm to me or to others?* If there is a better path, shouldn't a wise person follow it? The *Bible* urges, "...let us throw off everything that hinders and the sin that so easily entangles, and let us run with perseverance the race marked out for us" *(Hebrews 12:1).*

Too much religious and subjective *Bible*-thumping for you? Then let's look at it scientifically and objectively. Albert Einstein wrote, "The significant problems we face cannot be resolved at the same level of thinking we were at when we created them." Some people say the definition of insanity is making the same mistake again and again but expecting a different outcome. Both statements say the same thing: the problems created by our patterns of behavior won't be solved by applying the same old patterns even more intensely. We need the sane solution of a reasonable response.

Life's living option

We're about to move on but before we do, I want you to know about what William James called "Life's Living Option." He said that in all of life's events, each of us has choices to make. Furthermore, he observed that:

- We have the ability to make a choice.
- There is a consequence to our choice.
- While we are choosing, we are in one of our choices.

For example, a man is in a stalled car sitting on a railroad crossing. He hears a train's whistle close by. Suddenly, he is in Life's Living Option. He has a choice—to stay in the car or get out.

- He has the ability to make the choice.
- There is a consequence to his choice—life if he gets out, death if he stays in.
- While he is choosing, he is still in the car!

If a woman has been diagnosed with a fatal disease that can be successfully treated only by her surgeon, she is in Life's Living Option. She has a choice—to submit to the uncertainties of surgery and probably live or to avoid the surgery and certainly die.

- She has the ability to choose.
- There is a consequence to her choice—life if she has the surgery, death if she does not.
- While she is choosing, she is already dying!

In terms of behavior and personal style, you are in Life's Living Option. You have a choice to make. You can continue exercising your *strengths,* excusing your *weaknesses,* and neglecting your *struggles,* or you can choose to say, "I will do what is necessary to maximize my God-given design and potential."

- Given the information you now possess, you have the ability to make either choice.
- You understand the consequences of your choice— enhanced living if you move ahead, diminished results if you continue living strictly through your own filters.
- While you are choosing, you are in one of your choices. You are doing what you have always done, but expecting that it will someday bring what has eluded you.

This is your *moral* decision. Will you stay where you are—unadjusted and often inappropriate—or will you combine your new knowledge with your considerable life experience to create higher levels of success for yourself and others? What will you do with your Divine Design?

Are you thinking, "Wait a minute—I didn't sign up to change my life, just to read a book"? That's fair. You bought this book with the idea of making your life more harmonious and productive. You're looking for ways to make your personal and professional relationships work more easily. I haven't pulled a bait-and-switch on you at all. I just want you to think about this: when you commit to living what you're reading, you will achieve what you're after.

I believe that once I learned these truths, I became obligated to protect myself, and those important to me, by moving beyond the limitations of my *natural* style.

It is morally right to become better.

Chapter 12:
Learn to Discern

Mark Twain explained a key difference between animals and people: both can *learn,* but people can *learn to discern.* He said that a cat sitting on a hot stove will learn instantly not to do it ever again. However, that "smart" cat will never again sit on a cold stove, either!

Many of our clashes with other people are based in issues of style, whether we recognize the issues or not. It's natural for us to slap a label on those "disagreeable" individuals who are "mean," "immature," "spineless," or "picky." We base our labels on how we view the appropriateness of *their* style... through the filter of *our own* style.

The truth is that people of any style can respond very appropriately at one time, but very inappropriately at other times. So, when we cross someone off our list as having little value, based on their reactions in a certain situation, we are behaving like the cat that couldn't distinguish between a cool stove ("safe" or "good") and a hot stove ("dangerous" or "bad").

We can't avoid friction as we work together. However, we can become "people smart" by understanding the style filters through which others perceive life and its challenges. Then we will understand that people don't do things *against* us, but *for themselves.* And we'll be able to appreciate and tap into their admirable qualities.

Great expectations

Often our frustration and anger over situations happen because our expectations were not met. We anticipated a particular response or outcome—then *zing!* It went flying out the window, taking our hopes and plans with it.

One of the greatest benefits of understanding behavior styles is being able to anticipate more of the cause-and-effect issues that surprise us. For instance:

- If you issue an ultimatum to someone with very intense **D** traits, should you really be surprised to encounter opposition? Of course not! **D**s seem to thrive on conflict and should be expected to rise to the occasion!

- If you assign a long-term task to someone with very intense **I** traits, but don't establish deadlines and account-ability measures along the way, should you be surprised if the person's time slips away and the project falls behind? No—**I**s can be distracted easily by people and events and are not typically long-range planners.

- If you give the task of deciding who gets promoted and who gets laid off in your business to someone with very intense **S** traits, should you be surprised to see them crumble under the pressure? No—**S**s want to help and please everyone and might resign before accepting such a sensitive and difficult assignment.

- If you discover an accounting error made by someone with very intense **C** traits, should you be surprised if they seem insulted and defensive when you say, "Wow! What were you thinking when you let this one slip by?" No—many **C**s are perfectionists who view mistakes as personal flaws.

Unmet expectations create disappointment. If we expect those with different styles to respond as we would in every situation, we'll be disappointed by unmet expectations more often that not. Here are more "intelligent" actions concerning the previous examples, based on informed expectations:

- Knowing that a **D** type individual hears a challenge and sees a contest in almost every situation, you would not throw down a dare. Instead, you would enlist cooperation and compliance by presenting options and choices, along with "ownership" of the outcome.

- Knowing that an **I** type operates best in a people-oriented environment, you would provide incentives for progress and break the job down into a series of smaller tasks with frequent reporting and refocusing on the task.

- Knowing that **S** types will have difficulty wielding the downsizing ax, you would not burden them with making this decision alone. You would recognize their value in helping employees make the required transition and involve them in a team to make the best decisions. Then you would offer support and encouragement that good decisions were being made because of their contribution to the team effort.

- Knowing that a **C** type tends to view mistakes as failures, you would provide an opportunity for self-discovery of the error. Privately, rather than in front of others, you would say, "I didn't quite follow this part—maybe you should check this over one more time." Rather than feeling embarrassed and retreating from the team, **C**s will validate their accuracy by "discovering" their miscalculation and will learn that the rest of the team can accept imperfection.

Here is a key to unmet expectations: let's learn enough about the ways people behave to make sure our expectations are more accurate. We'll be much less frustrated when we see predictable patterns and understand what's happening behind the scenes.

Your adjusted style

Many of the assessment instruments that accurately report on your personal style show 2 graphs: one is your "natural," "core," "basic," or "unadapted" style—the *real* you. The other graph is your "adjusted," "environmental," or "adapted" style—how you "raise" and "lower" your *D, I, S,* and *C* traits to achieve and succeed in your environment.

Sometimes we adapt and adjust well. We borrow some supporting traits from our personal "blend" (see Chapter 9), and we boost their intensity to help us accomplish what is necessary. Sometimes our blend just doesn't provide what we need, and we must "synthesize" something that might work for us...temporarily!

The goal of adapting our style and adjusting our behavior is to respond appropriately. We need to *assess* our situation, *discern* the appropriate response, and then *use* the style traits and people skills at our disposal.

Most of us are capable of temporary adjustments, but stress builds when we have to make these adjustments for a longer period of time, or when we're tired or sick, or when other environmental pressures put us on edge. Then, we tend to drop the veneer and revert to our real selves, except that we're operating in survival mode! Because of this, we become more self-serving in our reactions.

The dangers of survival mode

I learned about survival mode when my wife endured 16½ hours of back labor, giving birth to our younger daughter, Danielle. Toward the end, she became highly focused on one objective: getting that baby born! Cindy's blood pressure had dropped very low and, as Danielle crowned, the obstetrician saw that the baby was face-up instead of face-down. Normally rational and cooperative, Cindy disregarded the doctor's instructions to lie back and rest as he tried to turn the baby. Cindy didn't argue with the doctor; she just kept pushing until she delivered her baby. No one could talk her into anything else—her survival mode was engaged. To her, it was the only rational thing to do. She knew her body and her child were in trouble, and she was going to do what was necessary. (By the way, she did the right thing. The doctor told us later that she could not have survived a last-minute C-section.)

When our personal styles switch to survival mode, the way we respond/react seems the only reasonable thing to do. Typically, we overreact; our *strengths* operate out of balance and truly become our *weaknesses*. (When we recognize this and begin bringing our *strengths* under control again, they become only *struggles!*) Until we see that we have been acting out of control, we won't recognize that we are losing credibility and respect.

In survival mode, each type tends to exhibit the *struggles* shown on Pages 63–66. While **DISC** is not a measure of our values, our behavior can be *others-focused* or *self-focused,* which is how many people interpret our values.

How and when to adjust

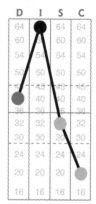

Using me as your guinea pig, let's look at my personal style chart *(right)*. It corresponds with a lot of the *I* traits found on Page 64. Because my *I* is so intense, I often *struggle* to control it. My normal tendency is to be off-the-wall, funny, friendly, irreverent, impulsive, emotional, open, trusting...we discussed these inclinations at length in Chapter 11. They are further intensified by the position of *C* in my chart. What *could* serve as a balance for my *I* traits has taken a holiday! Yet, much of the work I do requires attention to details—a *C* trait if ever there was one. What motivates me, and how do I do it?

1. *Is* tend to "perform" for recognition. Doing something poorly will never bring me the acknowledgment I want. If I am going to put my reputation on the line, I want to get the details right and not embarrass myself. My motivation is not the same as a true *C*'s, who thinks detail and accuracy are their own rewards.

2. My attention to detail will not be as consistent as a *C*'s because I am *"synthesizing"* it rather than drawing from my *natural strengths*. If I make a list to follow in completing my task, it's not because I love making lists. (Many *C* type people enjoy organizing things into lists and checking them off.) It's because I know people and events easily distract me from my tasks. Again, the list helps me look dutiful ("good") instead of forgetful ("bad").

3. I must have backup systems. My *I* traits are intense, and

most of my **C** traits are slight, so I know I can't accurately proofread my books and articles. I know that my imagination will "correct" whatever is wrong as I read, so most of my errors are not obvious to me. I know what it should say, so my mind agrees with me instead of the words on the page. My backup system includes people who proofread my work, and I come back to my work again after several days' absence if I want my own fresh perspective.

4. I keep a sense of humor about my struggle. Because I know attention to detail will always be a struggle for me—even though I work at improving and concentrating—I make sure I don't exhaust my batteries. I try to make time for what charges me up. For someone with lots of **I**, the battery-charger is *interaction* with people. If I reach a goal, I celebrate it before plunging into another task.

Each of us needs to learn how to do the 4 things listed above according to our style.

For example, someone with intense **C** traits and very few *I* traits could easily become frustrated in a job that requires lots of spontaneity. Their gifts and skills tend to fall into the reserved, cautious, plan-it-all-out category. Telling this person to be spontaneous is like telling *me* to be organized—we really would have to *think* about it! A **C** type's spontaneity may *appear* natural, but it's most likely well-rehearsed by the time you see it.

A great example of this was the comedic actress Lucille Ball, who entertained the world in *I Love Lucy*. She seemed to be the dizzy, spontaneous *I* type who always spoke before thinking, but she was really the highly detailed genius behind

Desilu Studios, which produced her TV show. I read that when she had to do a scene with Vivian Vance, the actress who played her best friend Ethel, Lucy hid herself away for several hours in her dressing room with a stack of paper bags. The script called for Lucy to burst a blown-up bag behind Ethel, scaring her to cure her hiccups. Lucy didn't emerge from her dressing room until she had discovered exactly how much air, blown into a paper bag of specific size, would create just the right "pop" to make the scene as funny as possible to the live audience in the studio and the people watching at home.

We could call this "planned spontaneity." I know a successful seminar leader who has lots of fun with her audience, even though her *I* traits are much less intense than her *C* traits. How does she do it? She *plans* her "spontaneous" fun down to the last detail!

As another example, I know a consultant who has very high *C* traits, while his people-oriented *I* and *S* traits barely register on his personal style graph. Yet he is warm and personable with clients and friends. I once asked him how he was able to be so consistent in displaying traits that aren't natural strengths. He replied, "I had a problem with that until some friends demonstrated to me the *value* of relationships." Do you see? He is not warm and friendly because it flows out of him automatically, as with many *I* and *S* type people. Instead, he sees these traits as worthwhile because someone offered *evidence* that *proved* to him the *value* of relating successfully to people. He has learned to "speak the language."

We can all learn to do things that are not natural to our style. Our motivation doesn't have to match everyone else's.

We all tend to do things for our own reasons anyhow. When should we adapt and adjust? When it is necessary, required, or appropriate to do so.

Natural versus adapted style

Allow me another personal example of the differences between our *natural* and *adapted* styles. I love meeting new people, having new experiences, doing unusual things, and then being able to *talk* and *talk* and *talk* about them with others. My *I* gift for gab and outgoing disposition have made it possible for me to meet many famous people, and I'm a confirmed name-dropper.

If I were invited to a formal dinner at the White House, you know I would attend with the anticipation of coming home with some great stories to tell. I would be thinking of all the clever and cordial things I could say to the President in the receiving line. I would make an impression on him, and he would remember me! This would probably be my motivation for attending. Certainly, I wouldn't be motivated by the food I would eat, although I *could* be demotivated by it.

One of the few foods I dislike is mushy, boiled asparagus. You can hide it under cheese, sprinkle it with breadcrumbs, or bury it in a casserole—I'll find it and dislike it. So how would I feel if I were seated at dinner and the White House staff served me a huge bowl of mushy, boiled cream of asparagus soup? Because it was the White House, I could make adjustments, couldn't I? I would eat it. But I would not enjoy it!

Meanwhile, I would quickly look around the table to see what other options were available. Perhaps another table was being served an entree unaccompanied by this green goo. No luck—they had just been served large platters of mushy, boiled asparagus spears. The ALABAMA ASSOCIATION OF ASPARAGUS ADVOCATES was totally responsible for the evening's repast! I wouldn't want to appear unsophisticated, ungrateful, or impolite. So I would put a small amount on my plate and nibble at it passively. But I would be drawing on all the adapting and adjusting skills I possess. This was not what I expected, and I would be disappointed. But what a great story I would tell my friends about the great time I had trading ideas with The Prez!

And of course, on the way home, I would find a store that sold chocolate Dove Bars so I could recharge my batteries and reenergize myself.

We have all spent time doing things that were necessary to our work or relationships, even though we didn't really enjoy doing them. We did those things for "the cause," or because is was part of the assignment, or to please someone else. We adapted and adjusted.

Sometimes we get so accustomed to adapting and adjusting to our "mushy, boiled asparagus" that we forget what our "Dove Bar" tastes like. Perhaps your work has elements that put you under stress, but you've been eating "boiled asparagus" at your job for so long that you've become accustomed to living that way. One of the great things that understanding your style can provide for you is a new set of taste buds—a hunger for work that tastes good to you, rather than the leftovers of life to which you've become accustomed.

Many times, companies experience marked increases in productivity when their employees have completed a Personal Style Assessment because the employees have gone back to work with a renewed understanding of their value to the team. They've discovered what they're good at, what's worth celebrating, so they improve what they do and how they do it.

Recharging our batteries

You have probably experienced periods of adjustment that left you drained of energy.

- If **D** traits are your most intense, you will be deenergized by passive activities and recharged by physical activity.
- If **I** traits are your most intense, you will be deenergized by isolation and recharged by social time.
- If **S** traits are your most intense, you will be deenergized by frenetic emotional times and recharged by "nothing" time.
- If **C** traits are your most intense, you will be deenergized by large crowd activities and recharged by private time.

In order to stay out of your survival mode, you need to nurture and protect your vulnerabilities. These are the *strengths* you have that can be abused, and they are the areas from which you have little to draw—especially in your "opposite" style. Here are 2 quick examples:

1. As I'm writing this book, we make our home with 4 generations: my wife and me, our 2 children, their grandmother, and their great-grandmother, who is 96 years old. That's a lot of people under one roof, a lot of coming and going, a lot of noise, a lot of mess. My wife has very strong **C** traits— orderliness is a big deal to her. She says cleanliness is next to godliness. I say godliness is next to impossible—so cleanliness is next to next to impossible!

Clutter has a physical impact on my wife; it can make her physically ill. She has filing systems; I have piling systems. You don't see her often in my home office, The Dungeon, because of the unstructured way I work. But you will find her in her quiet space, a room where she can get away from all the demands of being a stay-at-home mom for 4 generations. This is where she recharges herself—not because she doesn't love us, but so she is able to love us better.

2. I attended a training session several years ago for entrepreneurs and wannabe business owners. In an attempt to stir them to action, a **D** speaker told the crowd that if they were winners—if they were going to succeed—the first day they returned home, they would contact 20 new prospects. When they heard this, the **S** types in the audience sighed with dismay. While his comments were deenergizing to **S**s, just being in this much excitement, noise, and energy was deenergizing them anyway. In order to succeed at their business, the first thing they needed to do when they got home was take a 2-day nap!

Here's a key to avoiding survival mode: *learn to discern* how to keep your batteries charged. There are things you can do physically, socially, emotionally, and spiritually to keep yourself energized. Understanding the energy needs of your personal style will help you stay at your best. Protect your vulnerabilities so you will have energy to adapt and adjust appropriately.

Chapter 13:
Reading Styles
at a Glance

All the information you've read so far is good to know, but you won't have much success beginning conversations by saying, "Can you take a few minutes and fill out this questionnaire for me? I'd like to submit your responses to a guy in Atlanta who wrote a book about personal style behaviors and preferences. He can run you through his computer and tell me what type you are. It could take a couple of days to get the results back, but then I'll know how to adapt and adjust in our relationship, so hold that thought till I get back to you!"

It is invaluable to know the kind of information contained in the computerized report. It provides many amazing insights for the individual who is the focus of the assessment and for those the results are shared with. I recommend it enthusiastically for everyone who lives or works in close relationships with others. But, you also need a set of tools you can use on the spot. Because **DISC** is an observable language, there is much you can *infer* to set you on course for success by *observing* friends, relatives, sales prospects, students, patients, managers, supervisors, employees, coworkers, and others. The following pages include some observable signs you can look for.

This is the *first* sign to notice on anyone you meet. It won't be quite as obvious with some as with others, but everyone wants to be treated this way. No one wants to be treated as an object. Most of us are keenly aware of the need to determine whether the individuals we deal with care about *people* and use *things,* or whether they care about *things* and use *people.* The best way to convince people that we value their *worth* more than their *work* is to treat them according to the *needs* and *wants* of their personal style.

This is also a good place to note that what you observe about a person's style is confidential information. *In most circumstances, you should not volunteer your observations to anyone, including that individual!* Here are a few reasons:

1. Some people resent the idea that another person can know so much about them. Most of us think we conceal our true emotions and have no idea how transparent we are.

2. Some people fear that information like this can be used to manipulate them, or take unfair advantage. It's like the guy who knows a couple of amazing card tricks winning too often at poker—he's sometimes suspected of cheating.

3. The purpose of this information is to help you adapt and adjust your own style so you can be more effective in working with others, not to show off how smart you are.

4. You'll find yourself dragged into issues about which you have no authority to speak. Keep your secret identity—even Superman could be Clark Kent most of the time!

DESCRIPTIVE WORD			
DOMINANCE Bold, adventurous, competitive	**INFLUENCE** Animated, inspiring, motivating	**STEADINESS** Loyal, faithful, compassionate	**COMPLIANCE** Reserved, disciplined, controlled
BASIC STYLE'S NEEDS & MOTIVATORS			
CONTROL choice, challenge, authority, variety, freedom, prestige	**RECOGNITION** acceptance, interaction, approval, fun, status	**APPRECIATION** assurance, closure, inclusion, specialization, harmony	**INFORMATION** accuracy, logic, procedures, value, security
STYLE SYMBOL (see Pages 102–105)			
OVEN MITT sometimes too hot to handle	**FIRECRACKER** unpredictable excitement	**SAFETY PIN** undercover helper, sharpness covered	**MAGNIFIER** attention to details
LIFE QUESTION			
WHAT? the bottom line, results	**WHO?** peer recognition, reward	**HOW?** defined measures of performance	**WHY?** objectives, predefined standards
BODY LANGUAGE			
EXPANSIVE HAND GESTURES authoritative	**MANY FACIAL EXPRESSIONS** and hand gestures	**HAND GESTURES** small gestures	**FEW HAND GESTURES** very controlled
BODY POSTURE			
LEAN FORWARD in charge, hand in pocket	**FEET APART** casual, both hands in pockets	**LEAN BACK** peaceful, a hand in a pocket	**FOLD ARMS** thoughtful, hand on chin
CONVERSATIONAL STYLE			
DIRECT results-oriented, flat statements, prefers to multitask on projects	**TALKATIVE** personal, confidential, easily sidetracked, expressive tones	**WARM** friendly, concerned, unhurried, good listener	**CLARIFYING** businesslike, questioning, fact-based, monotone

PREFERRED VEHICLE TYPE

POWERFUL	SHOWY	PRACTICAL	VALUE
status-oriented, prestige package, luxury options	colorful, novel (a red convertible?), attractive	comfortable, with room for others	good economy, whether luxury or compact

RESPONSE TO A TARGET

READY...	READY...	READY...	READY...
FIRE...	AIM...	READY...	AIM...
AIM....	TALK....	READY...	AIM...
		READY....	AIM....

PREFERRED READING MATERIALS

SUMMARIES	IMPROVEMENT	PEOPLE STORIES	TECHNICAL
book abridgements, reviews, notes, money/success	self-help books, adventure fiction, people/psych	fiction or non, "Chicken Soup," home/hospitality	journals, how-to, history, nonfiction, consumer

BLIND SPOT & FEAR

FEELINGS OF OTHERS	KEEPING COMMITMENTS	AWARENESS OF TIME PRIORITY	THE OVERVIEW OR BIG PICTURE
being used unfairly by others	loss of social acceptance	confrontation and change in routine	unpredictable outcomes, risk

SELF-ORGANIZATION

EFFICIENT	DISORGANIZED	ORGANIZED	HIGH
functional and uncomplicated; not neat	intuitive and unstructured; piles, not files	practical and simple; a little sloppy	detailed systems and categories; neat

PURCHASING PATTERN

QUICK DECISION	IMPULSIVE	SLOW DECISION	CAUTIOUS
likes the new and unique, solution-oriented	likes the new and unique, showy-oriented	likes the familiar and established, tradition-oriented	likes the tried and proven, quality-oriented

RECHARGING ACTIVITY

ACTIVE	INTERACTIVE	RESTFUL	SOLITARY
seeks physical exertion and competition	seeks activity with people in distractive fun	seeks passive rest or sleep, even hot baths	seeks quiet time alone with thoughts

SOME FAVORED OCCUPATIONS

ATHLETE	SALESPERSON	REMODELER	ENGINEER
ENTREPRENEUR	PERFORMER	DIPLOMAT	ACCOUNTANT
DIRECTOR	INSTRUCTOR	TEACHER	RESEARCHER
LAW OFFICER	PROMOTER	CARE PROVIDER	PROGRAMMER

PRODUCTIVE ENVIRONMENT

REWARDS FOR RESULTS	HIGH PEOPLE CONTACT	ESTABLISHED METHODS	REWARDS FOR QUALITY
non-routine and innovative tasks	networking, widely varying tasks	predictability and close teamwork	specialization, quiet, small group

FAVORED WORKSPACE

POWERFUL	CONTEMPORARY	PERSONAL	FUNCTIONAL
efficient, with large desk	showy, with life memorabilia	homelike, with family artifacts	impersonal, with charts and graphs

RESPONSE TO AUTHORITY

RULE BREAKER	UNAWARE	SUBJECTIVE	COMPLIANT
questions rules; believes the end justifies the means	asks forgiveness rather than permission	follows rules that make sense and are time-proven	knows and follows all rules and expects others to

RESPONSE TO CONFLICT

AGGRESSES	EVADES	TOLERATES	AVOIDS
resists opposition and wants to win at any cost	may seem fearful and easily feels rejection	hides emotions rather than confronting	may give in rather than oppose others

RESPONSE TO CHANGE

INSTIGATING	UNAWARE	OPPOSED	CONCERNED
thrives on change and takes on new challenges	may not perceive; then will seek a role and inclusion	passively opposes; needs advance warning to prepare	cautious about the impact and effect of change

WANTS A LEADER WHO IS

GOAL-ORIENTED	DEMOCRATIC	EASYGOING	DETAIL-ORIENTED
direct, challenging, rewards personal accomplishment	friendly, sociable, offers short-term incentives	defines goals and offers support for reaching them	seeks feedback, has high standards, plans long-term

A symbol for understanding Ds...

Developing word pictures helps solidify a concept in our minds. This image captures both the *strengths* and *struggles* of the dominating **D** type:

If you want to get a project cooking, give it to a *fast-paced, task-oriented D.* They know how to turn up the heat! When you do this to *projects,* they get well-done, but when you turn up the heat on *people,* they get burned.

The flaming **OVEN MITT** reminds **Ds** to watch their heat carefully—and reminds others that they sometimes need heat protection.

With all of the **D**'s wonderful traits, sometimes they can be too hot to handle. When we get burned by their intensity, we *can* respond with an attitude that the risk of being burned again is too great—as the cat decides that all stoves should be avoided in the future. Or we can *learn to discern:*

We can handle **Ds** more cautiously. Don't be surprised or intimidated when they challenge your statements or automatically assume control. A wise **D** will recognize this heat tendency and either turn it down or find ways to insulate others from it. When things begin to heat up, create insulation from the **D**'s intensity by anticipating inappropriate responses and controlling a more appropriate environment.

A symbol for understanding *Is*...

This image captures both the *strengths* and *struggles* associated with the spontaneous *I* type:

If you want to guarantee variety and excitement, include a *fast-paced, people-oriented I*—you never know what will happen! No one will be ignored, and the team will bond together.

The **FIRECRACKER** reminds us to be careful when and where *Is* are allowed to go off! In the right place, they create amazement and celebration; in the wrong place, only distraction and destruction result.

With all of the *I's* wonderful traits, sometimes they can be too spontaneous and unpredictable. When we get blown up by their impulsiveness, we *can* respond with an attitude that the risk of being blown up again is too great. We can avoid all *Is* in the future. Or we can *learn to discern:*

We can handle *Is* more tactfully when they start sparking. Don't be surprised or intimidated by their excitability or emotionalism. A wise *I* will recognize this tendency and either snuff the fuse or discover other ways and safer places to spark. Channel their energy and enthusiasm by anticipating their responses and creating a more appropriate environment for everyone.

A symbol for understanding Ss...

Again, strong word pictures solidify concepts in our minds. This image captures both the *strength* and *struggles* of the supportive **S** type:

Ss expect loyalty and fairness from others. They may not often express their true feelings when upset or unappreciated, but they can carry a grudge if mistreated.

The **SAFETY PIN** reminds us that **S**s prefer working out of sight and undercover and while they have the capability to respond sharply to others, they usually keep their pointed responses and attitudes covered up.

With all of the **S**'s wonderful traits, sometimes they can be too quiet, voicing their important feelings and opinions only with close and trusted friends. When they finally react with a sharp, pointed response, we *can* respond with an attitude that the risk of being pricked again is too great. Or we can *learn to discern:*

We can handle **S**s more sensitively by taking time to *listen carefully* to the attitudes and responses they tend to stuff inside. A wise **S** will recognize this tendency and either learn to speak up...or go take it out on Mark Twain's cat! We can deal with them personally and honestly, creating a more aware and conducive environment for working together.

A symbol for understanding Cs...

This image captures both the *strengths* and *struggles* of the inquisitive and precise **C** type:

If you want assured accuracy and precise details, entrust your project to slower-paced, task-oriented **C**s. They have been known to proofread a handful of *M&Ms!* (After all, a "W" might try to sneak in somewhere!) Their identity and self-image are tied to their sense of correctness.

The **MAGNIFYING GLASS** reminds **C**s to watch out for the debilitating disease of "detail-itis"—and reminds the rest of us of the wisdom in double-checking even the obvious!

With all the **C**'s wonderful traits, sometimes they can become too focused on perfection, failing to recognize excellence in themselves and others. When we feel that we will never meet their standards, we *can* respond with an attitude that the risk of being made to feel inferior is too great. Or we can *learn to discern:*

We can handle **C**s more logically when working together, rather than being intimidated by their cold analysis. A wise **C** will recognize this tendency and either suspend fault-finding or develop warmer methods. We can anticipate their need for data and logic and, by responding appropriately, we can create an environment that is harmonious for all.

The charts in this chapter have been prepared so they can be studied in 2 ways: you can read *across* each topic, comparing and contrasting differences in style, or you can read *down* a list to develop a keen sense about one particular style. Once you become familiar with style characteristics, you will be able to read people more quickly and accurately, either by process of elimination or by observing the the identifying traits. In the former, you may observe a *lack* of certain behaviors that indicates less intensity—perhaps an individual does not exhibit a lot of **C** traits, for example. In the latter, you may identify stronger intensity—an individual seems to exhibit a lot of **S** traits instead.

The 4 symbols (oven mitt, firecracker, safety pin, and magnifying glass) should provide you with several keys for successful interaction:

- what to expect when individuals are under control
- what to expect when individuals are out of control
- how to respond appropriately to the individual's style
- how others may see you at times
- how you can adjust your behavior for better success in your personal and professional relationships

Let's be clear. The goal of this style-reading information is not to help you become only a "thermometer" that can measure the temperature of a particular situation or environment. The goal is to help you become a "thermostat" that can sense the temperature and then take action to adjust the environment so everyone can be more comfortable.

Chapter 14:
Thinking Out
of the Box

I think you will enjoy where this chapter takes us. We'll deal with the questions often asked by people discovering personal styles for the first time: "Aren't we putting labels on people? Aren't we limiting people by putting them in boxes?"

These are fair questions and, honestly, it's a temptation to do this when first learning these concepts. But the purpose of *D*, *I*, *S*, and *C* *labeling* has nothing to do with *disabling* growth or personal development (what Maslow called self-actualization). People want to be empowered to grow, and they want to be seen as individuals, not as subsets of a group. The purpose of the *DISC* language is to help us recognize and honor individuals and their differences so we can adapt and adjust ourselves for better, more successful relationships.

Aren't we putting people in boxes? No, they came that way—prepackaged! If anything, we're *opening up* the boxes they are already in.

Of course, some people are very happy to be in their boxes and want to keep them sealed tightly. The thought that you have been prying or snooping around in their box can be alarming, and this is why I suggest that you not make a big deal out of being able to "read" them or their personal style.

I've read that psychologist Alfred Adler said, "I don't put people in boxes—I just keep *finding* them there!" Style-wise, what kinds of boxes are people in? Some have open boxes and a healthy self-image that is not intimidated by this information. They like discovering themselves! Others may have lower self-esteem, but want to find ways to package themselves more appropriately. Still others may be more sensitive to the way they are perceived and require a cautious and careful approach in dealing with their boxes.

Honor the box and what's in it

Picture this scene: an intensely *I* type man is in charge of a project. He really wants to get it finished—it stopped being fun and became work a long time ago. Being *fast-paced* and *people-oriented*, attention to detail is not his strength. For balance, his people-smart manager has paired him with a coworker who has strong **C** traits and expects precision and perfection. They are opposites in so many ways and, not knowing about personal styles or how to adjust to work together productively, they get on each other's nerves.

This team's final report is due, and all the *I* wants is to sign off on it and get it to the manager's office. He's planning to make a verbal report anyhow, and he sees the written report as only a backup for his persuasive skills. His team partner has been working on charts and graphs, footnotes and appendices—her Executive Summary is longer than *his* presentation! As he sees her standing by the copy machine, proofreading again, he explodes in frustration. "Loosen up! You're not going to approve this document until it's on the *New York Times* best-seller list, are you? I ran it through spell-check after the first draft!"

Is the *I* team leader going to get what he wants by telling the *C* that "close is good enough"? As far as she is concerned, "a miss is as good as a mile." By dishonoring her need for accuracy, he is sending her a message that he approves of inaccuracy, and he drives her to protect even more what is vitally important in her eyes. In effect, he's saying, "Get out of your box," and she's replying, "Not a chance! If I leave my box unguarded, you'll come over and stomp it flat! You will destroy everything precious in it if you can. I'm staying in here and protecting it from you!" (Maslow's theory tells us that when her security and safety needs are threatened in this way, she will become more guarded and less open.)

As another example, a friend told me about scoring a touchdown while playing high school football against his team's crosstown rival. He was so proud, and he wanted recognition and acknowledgment from his coach. This would have been a major motivator because of his strong *I* traits, but the coach had intense *D* and *C* traits. He mistakenly thought praise would cause my friend to become self-satisfied and complacent—and he viewed congratulations as flattery. So, his single, unemotional comment was, "You know, if you'd tried harder, you could have made *2* touchdowns!" Did this pull my friend out of his box and encourage him? No, his excitement and reward were denied. He felt cheated, and the sport he loved began looking more like work and less like fun.

If your desire is to build mutual trust with those of differing styles, honor what comes in their boxes. You'll put joy back into their game but, more important, you'll contribute to their sense of safety, belonging, and esteem.

Once trust is established, you may see people venture out of their box from time to time. And if they know you'll be careful with what they find most valuable, they may even invite you *inside* their box occasionally. It's a special privilege when those who are very different from you bring you into their inner circle.

Characters and their characteristics

Sometimes appearances are intentionally deceptive. Superficial observation may mislead you as you try to read someone's style. The more information you have about that individual, and the more familiar you are with the chart descriptions in Chapter 13, the more accurate you will be.

I think I'm good at cold-reading people and their styles but, periodically, I'm reintroduced to reality when I miss key factors. Once, after a seminar for several thousand people, a man asked me if I could guess his style. I wanted to see him in action, so we talked about his life. He asked if I was familiar with the botanical sculptures at Walt Disney World—large shrubs in the shapes of famous Disney cartoon characters. I said yes. He replied that he lived in Orlando, designing and executing those displays for the park.

He was dressed conservatively, his reddish hair complemented by a tailored, sharply pressed, 4-button olive suit, with an earthtone tie, oxblood shoes and matching belt. He delivered his information in monotone with the controlled gestures of an engineer. Everything about him confirmed that he was a reserved, task-oriented **C**. I said so. And he giggled. His eyes began to sparkle and dance. His eyebrows quivered and arched as he exclaimed, "Nope—I'm an **I**!"

I was stunned. "Who dressed you this morning?" I asked, and he chirped, "My wife! She's the **C**!" The next time I saw him, he had dressed himself, and I could tell. He could play a **C**, but not for long!

Never judge a book by its cover

The back cover of this book lists a cast of characters with whom you come in contact every day in your personal and professional life. However, some are more complex than they appear on the surface, and it's easy to misjudge them. To bring out their best—or at least minimize the struggles as you team together—you need to understand their motivations, wants, and needs. So think of the next few pages of pictures and descriptions as a *recreational game*. Since you and I can't go to the mall together and watch the passing parade of interesting people, I've brought them to you for a closer look!

Being a people watcher is fun. It has become almost a hobby for me now, trying to figure out styles by watching people in action. The following pages are just for fun, but they will give you ideas about looking beyond the obvious, thinking about others' motivations as you build your people skills.

If the person you're observing has a very strong self-image and exhibits little in the way of self-doubt, you are probably dealing with a fast-paced, outgoing, extroverted type, like a **D** or an **I**. The other styles tend to call less attention to themselves, and they are usually not so quick to jump in and impose their solution on every crisis. *I* types tend to enjoy the limelight of being **THE HERO**, but not the controversy that comes with the cape. In the long run, this is a role **D** types relish, but they should be sure those they "rescue" truly want their help.

If the person you're observing has a spontaneous and impulsive sense of humor, you are probably dealing with a fast-paced, outgoing, extroverted, people-oriented **I** type. Their funny comments are sometimes inappropriate, and they use humor to handle awkward or sensitive situations. So, their anything-for-a-laugh guise of **THE CLOWN** may be hiding pain or discomfort. There are also **S** and **C** types who let go of their shyness through performing and entertaining, but a telling difference is in the amount and degree of spontaneity they reveal.

If the person you're observing works in the caring professions of nursing, teaching, and social services, they probably have a slower-paced, reserved, introverted **S** or **C** style. They follow details, achieve accuracy, adhere to procedures, and take time to provide proper service. Apart from professions, however, those who live **THE CAREGIVER** lifestyle tend to be people-oriented **S** types. Sometimes their efforts are misspent in projects that are on life-support because of loyalty to others and their desire to finish what they have started. It is hard for them to understand that their caring and sincere desire to help are not always an adequate prescription or cure.

If the person you're observing obsesses about details and is very cautious about committing to plans or programs before double-checking all the facts, you are dealing with someone who exhibits many **C** type traits. They do not always enjoy being **THE BOOKKEEPER**, but they sense that no one will ensure accuracy if they don't worry or obsess about it. They are probably correct about that too! If you don't value this trait in them, they will become even more concerned about your inattention to facts and figures. Don't tolerate or eliminate their energies and efforts in this direction. Instead, celebrate and liberate them to do what you probably dislike doing.

If the person you're observing enjoys keeping you off-balance and off-guard by changing plans and expectations without your knowledge, you're dealing with a task-oriented, independent **D** type who wants to maintain control. A question to consider is whether the **MYSTERY PERSON** uses this disinformation as a control tool. Sometimes people who are simply reserved, quiet **S**s and **C**s value their privacy, respect yours, and just want to do what's required without a lot of distraction or conflict, so don't misjudge. **I** types aren't like this at all. They are more expressive and transparent, showing their agenda rather than being so tactical.

If the person you're observing seems to have let life pass by and is oblivious to developing trends or issues many of us think are relevant, you may have stumbled over **THE SLEEPER**. Books like this one tend to picture **C** type people as sharp and very systematic. **C**s who fall outside this mold are often misunderstood. Einstein, for example, was considered retarded because he didn't speak until he was 4. This math wizard never memorized his telephone number because it was readily available in the directory. But he was a **C** in ways that mattered — complying with rules that were important to follow and wasting little thought or effort on the rest.

If the person you're observing speaks about the "unfairness" of a situation, thinking that they always win unless someone has cheated, you may be experiencing a peculiarity among **D** types. Perhaps because of their lack of self-doubt and capability, they expect to win every time. When they don't, **THE CONTENDER** expresses loudly that they would have if things were fair! A different view may come with maturity, but this is a role played by some highly competitive people who can't figure out why they lost, unless they were sucker-punched. It is an attempt to get a do-over. On the playground, you'll hear this complaint from young **D** children—at a good time to outgrow it.

If the person you're observing seems to live without accountability and is able to ask for forgiveness instead of permission, you are probably dealing with someone who has a lot of **I** traits—with some **D** type chutzpah! **THE CHARMER** is particularly aggravating to **C** types who always play by the rules. Part of the struggle for this style is that they have never really been bitten as the result of "charm" failure. When that eventually happens, they will need you to explain cause and effect while helping them recover. All of us should know how to charm a serpent occasionally, but there is never wisdom in tormenting snakes. Help them learn about consequences, but don't enjoy seeing them in pain.

If the person you're observing insists on perfection but is slow to compliment or forgive, they are trapped in being **THE LAWMAKER**. This often involves intense **C** traits. The person sees inconsistency all around and has not received recognition for playing by the rules. (On a bad day, when our wants are ignored, all of us want to lay down the law!) It is not a happy role for anyone. If this is a regular pattern, see what you can do to make these people feel more like insiders than outsiders. Simply flaunting the law will never make it go away.

If the person you're observing is creative, that alone provides no clue as to what style that person has! **D** types create vision and opportunity. **I** types create imagination and fantasy. **S**s create comfort and beauty. **C**s often create and standardize forms that already exist. So, **THE CREATIVE ARTIST** includes impressionists, realists, visionaries—even cartoonists! Creative artists can be sculptors who remove what is unnecessary or inventors who observe principles and improve ideas. Emotional sensitivity often accompanies creative effort, regardless of style. To be understood, carefully express yourself in the language of this person's observable style, and encourage their creativity.

If the person you're observing is always peering beyond the accepted facts of a situation, answer their "why" question. You're dealing with **THE SEEKER**, who naturally possesses intense **C** traits. Sometimes they appear as suspicious, but they really just want to shine light into the darkness. Their desire is not to catch you in error (like The Lawmaker), or even to assure a particular outcome (like The Bookkeeper). They have a consuming (sometimes overzealous) need to know. Their questions can seem trivial, but they may be putting solutions together in their minds. If they overwhelm you, challenge them to find answers instead of just asking you for information.

If the person you're observing seems too innocent to be true, don't automatically assume that they're being phony or deceptive. Those who look for a rainbow often seem to find it, while the rest of us are trying to protect them from the "real" world. **THE GOOD FAIRY** gives generously, not for acceptance or satisfaction, but from a value base that ranks people high above things. Those who are married to these men and women frequently say they didn't believe such people existed anymore...until they met their mates. Some people try to fake it but, over time, you can see the real ones shine.

If the person you're observing sees their environment as hostile and needing to be controlled and dominated, you're watching **THE LIONTAMER** in action. Cracking their whip, they seem to have a lot of **D** type traits. But this is not indicative of all **D**s. Sometimes a person has learned that this is "how it's always done," like old-time circus performers who would never go into the cage without their whips! This might be a **D**, or it could be an **I**, an **S**, or a **C** who has never seen problems resolved in any other manner. You can introduce them to the value of kitty treats!

If the person you're observing is calling all the shots and refusing input, they feel strong ownership and distrust the team's ability to succeed without their control. **THE DIRECTOR** wants to do it all—and perceives no possibility of worthwhile contributions from the crew, the cast, or even the star players. (This self-made person might better succeed in directing cartoon characters. They are more manageable than people and can be made to do exactly as desired.) In "real" Hollywood, it's the producer who controls the purse strings and therefore controls The Director. In your scenario, enlist the support of whoever has that authority, rather than attempting to sabotage the set.

If the person you're observing doesn't catch on to habitual mistakes in judgment that are obvious to others, you're seeing **THE SLOW LEARNER**. They are not dunces at all. In fact, they tend to be impulsive, fast-paced people with intense **I** or **I/D** blended traits, who don't understand life until they experience it. Slower-paced people can't comprehend this. Their types don't want to experience life until they understand it! Teach these people to slow down and see what they are overlooking. Offer to be an early sounding board for their decisions. As they make the connection between actions and outcomes, they will learn to transfer such principles into everyday living.

If the person you're watching is highly observant and sensitive to change, you've probably been studied by **THE INSPECTOR** long before you began studying him or her. These are the **C** types whose energy surfaces when the hunt is on. More than pursuers of facts, they pursue truth, and they do well in research and investigation. If most **C** types ask "Why?," then this type is sure to ask, "Who-what-where-why-how?" To them, life is a puzzle or riddle to be solved. More than quality answers, they want solutions. As anyone who is familiar with Sherlock Holmes, Lieutenant Columbo, or Jessica Fletcher knows, it's better to give them the complete answer the first time they ask.

If the person you're observing is punctual, predictable, prim, and punctilious, get acquainted with **THE PROPER PERSON**. These are **C** type people of high standards. They are normally courteous as well. They tend not to impose their strict standards on others or look down on those who disagree, as The Lawmaker does, because they are essentially very private people. Their lives conform to standards rather than expectations, and they expect to be permitted their own privacy and customs, just as they extend that right to you. Displays of emotion unsettle them, but they appreciate practical demonstrations of gratitude and acknowledgment of their faithful performance of duty.

If the person you're observing is already finding possible locations for their memorial statues, you are around **THE PERFORMER**. They enjoy public displays in their honor, even if they must do it for themselves. Often shameless self-promoters, they may need to be reminded that "there is no 'I' in TEAM...'" This behavior is a variation on the **I** theme. These individuals are more impulsive than The Clown and are close cousins of The Charmer without the charm. Recognition, reward, and applause tend to be their drivers and, without them, the performance continues elsewhere with a new audience. Rather than a need for esteem, insecurity motivates them.

You may encounter many other characters as you observe the types, styles, and behaviors of people. Here are a few others to watch for:

THE GOOD SPORT *doesn't complain about being mistreated because these* **S** *types are team players. But they are Score Keepers too! One day, you'll discover you owe penalties of which you are unaware for fouls you have forgotten. Encourage an open-door policy for this person to bring up questions, attitudes, and feelings, so you can keep short accounts. Schedule time to listen without assigning blame or having distractions.*

THE BULL ARTIST *plays loosely with the truth. Not much explanation is needed here. With lots of show and flourish, they work for leverage and prestige. Typically, they have undisciplined* **I** *and* **D** *traits that crave approval or control. Recognize their achievement and reward their accomplishments in the real world, and tactfully double-check the results they report.*

People who believe they must carry all the weight and responsibility of an outcome—not just control of the project—are **THE STRONGMAN** *type. They need to learn the skills of teamwork that make the burden easier to carry. Sometimes, these people adopt a tough-as-nails approach because they believe a leader should never show anything but strength. They fail to recognize that significant leadership skills exist in every type and style.*

THE VICTIM *is frequently hurt in life and unknowingly enables abuse in unhealthy relationships. Harmful behavior can be inflicted on anyone who submits to it as a matter of style or culture—whether physical, emotional, or mental. (Personal style assessment has also been used to predict industrial safety problems. Style-related stress can make certain individuals more vulnerable to workplace injuries. This area is the subject of expanded data-gathering and research. If you are particular interested, I have additional information.)*

There are some people for whom **DISC** is not a valid measure of style. I am referring to the 5% or so in modern cultures who are **THE UNBALANCED**. (Remember that Marston's book was The Emotions of Normal People.) There are some individuals who can't be typed with this instrument, but can be measured in psychiatric terms. However, even in cultures that are much more reserved than ours, the 4-factor behavior model still holds true. For example, among female groups that are subservient to males in their society, all 4 styles manifest themselves when the females are among only culturally similar women. It is then that they demonstrate the range of **D, I, S,** and **C** behaviors.

On the subject of reformation, some people say, "I started out as a **C**, but now I'm an **I**." It doesn't work that way. Research shows that much of our style is preestablished and inherited. You can learn to adjust more appropriately for your environment, but the factors of PACE and PRIORITY are not yours to choose. The values that shape how you use your traits can change. If your values have caused you to misuse your traits—and you have earned **THE CROOK**'s reputation—know that your appropriate behavior, not your personal style, is the issue you must deal with. Behavior is the standard to use, and not a person's past, when commenting on their character.

If you could choose to be most like any character, the one to imitate is **THE MARKSMAN**. His skill is adjusting to changing conditions and consistently hitting the bull's-eye. Remember that the original definition of "sin" meant "missing the mark," so being on-target should be your aim. On-target means anticipating, understanding, and meeting the needs and wants of others appropriately. Doing this brings success in personal and professional relationships.

Putting your puzzle together

You don't have to know everything about personal styles to have better relationships but, when you have questions about yourself or others, style issues are a great place to start looking for answers.

My friend Lee Ellis, creator of the *Personality I.D.* system and the *RightPath4* assessment, has researched style issues and vocational choices extensively. The chart on Page 101 lists only a sampling of occupations in which different types may find success and enjoyment. Literally, there are *hundreds* of professions well suited to each type—I selected just a few. Note that in the **D** column, law enforcement is listed. It's not unusual for police work to be listed in the category of *fast-pace, task-oriented,* regardless of the name assigned to this type. (Many of the behavioral assessment companies listed on Pages 10 and 11 use other descriptive labels for **D** type behavior.)

Once, following a seminar, a man approached the presenter and said, "I notice on your occupational list that **D**s make good police officers. This has me wondering...I'm not a **D** at all—I'm a **C**. Do you think I'm in the wrong career?"

Sometimes answering a question with a question can give you time to think. The presenter was weighing options in his head. If the man served as a detective, **C** type traits would be handy. And in the traffic division, his accident investigation reports would be detailed and flawless. Of course, as a police records officer clerk, he could track evidence and reports, and he would probably know exactly where everything was. So, the presenter proceeded with his question: "Where do you serve on the police force?"

"I'm assigned to the SWAT Team," the officer replied.

"No wonder he's concerned," the presenter thought. "I can't imagine him battering his way through a door and commanding, 'Everybody get down on the floor—now!'"

So, the presenter asked, "What is it you do on the SWAT Team?"

And the officer replied, "I'm the sniper." Bulls-eye! Can you think of any other style you would rather have with their finger resting on the trigger? Wouldn't you want someone with lots of cautious, careful, correct, calculating **C** type traits? If you were trapped in a hostage situation with emotions running high, wouldn't you be thankful that the person who had the bad guy in his sites had grown up believing it was good to measure twice, cut once? In this situation, he would aim twice and shoot once, knowing this one shot had to count. (Dr. Robert Alan Black, who consults with chiefs of police across North America, tells me that intensely **C** type traits are desired in SWAT Team members, who, whatever their role, are expected *not to initiate* nor *act independently,* but to await a mastermind decision for the team.)

Sometimes a job and a person's style are not a good fit. Have you heard someone say, "He just wasn't the right *person* for the job"? It means the person and the demands of the project were not a good match. Rather than the *person* not being right, it might have been that the *job* wasn't right for that person. Don't let the perceived limitations of your style hold you back from following your passions! Understanding and compensating for your style's strengths and struggles may make it possible for you to succeed where others with similar styles have failed.

Some of our exercises with the *D, I, S,* and *C* symbols, the charts, and the characters in the last 2 chapters have been focused on making the types become more tangible and alive to you. They will become more and more real as you lift these ideas from the book and carry them out to work, to the mall, to the post office, to restaurants, to your place of worship, and back home.

Like with a puzzle, the more pieces you can see, the more you can visualize the completed image. The more pieces you can fit together, the sooner the puzzle can be solved.

SECTION IV: APPLICATIONS IN PERSONAL RELATIONSHIPS

Chapter 15:
Style in Marriage
Relationships

This chapter focuses on married couples, but don't flip past it if you are not someone's spouse. We'll be looking at situations that can occur in other relationships too. They just happen to fit better into this chapter than into the chapters about parenting and friendships with those outside of your immediate family.

Whoever said, "You can pick your friends, but you're stuck with your relatives" spoke volumes. Of course, so did the person who said, "Blood is thicker than water."

In some ways, our expectations are higher in dealing with family members. After all, love is "in spite of," not "because of." If anyone should understand us and make room for our foibles, it should be family. Instead, for many, family is the setting for displays of hostility that don't occur outside the home.

You married a stranger

What we have considered earlier about *unmet expectations* plays a major role in many disagreements and frustrations that spouses experience. In my own life, I had no understanding of what caused my wife to think and act as she did. Why wasn't she "normal," like me? I know she was thinking the same thing. "What is going on in his tiny mind?"

Of course, we didn't start out with these questions. Each of us thought the other was *wonderful!* Cindy's job was like a pressure cooker but, whenever we spoke, she found herself laughing and lighthearted within moments. In our premarriage relationship, I supplied an important release— I made her life *fun* again. For me, Cindy was a strong, expressive, self-sufficient woman who spoke her mind, who had things to do and places to go. We liked each other's families; they were very different from our own.

Have you figured it out yet? *Opposites attract.* Eventually, though, opposites *attack!* What was so fascinating before we said, "I do," became so predictable after our wedding.

In earlier chapters, we used the diagram below to show basic differences in the 4 types:

- *Thinking* versus *Relating*
- *Extroverted* versus *Introverted*
- *Antagonistic* versus *Favorable*
- *Active* versus *Passive*
- *Fast-paced* versus *Slower-paced*
- *Task-oriented* versus *People-oriented*

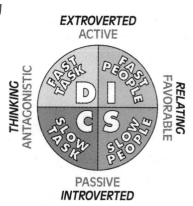

We said the type opposite your own is the one you probably understand least. But here is the key: *for many, this is also the style of the person we married!* We promised to spend our lives cherishing his or her differences. *What were we thinking?* To tell the truth, most of us weren't. Even highly logical, unemotional **C** type lovers can appreciate 17th Century mathematician and philosopher's Blaise Pascal's comment, "The heart has its reasons which reason does not know."

Until I got married, I didn't know there is *only one proper way* to load a dishwasher, but my wife has a lot of **C**, and she told me so. I didn't know anything about **C** when she was trying to teach me the dishwasher lesson, or it might have gone more smoothly for both of us.

I've mentioned that I have a "piling" system instead of a filing system in my office. Cindy can tolerate that because she doesn't deal with it on a daily basis, but my **I** traits tend to scatter all over the house. Until we learned about **DISC**, she thought I did this because I had no respect for her or the work she did to keep an orderly house. To her, orderliness is not a *habit*—it's a *way of life*. It is inborn, and anything less is foreign to her.

How did Cindy and I get to be the way we are? Did we pick what we tolerate and decide what irritates us? No. Research indicates that family members *inherit* some of their behavioral traits. Other traits are shaped in you through upbringing and environment. The former is *nature;* the latter is *nurture*.

Poor, sweet baby

There's a wonderful *Peanuts* comic strip that Cindy and I have laughed about. In it, Charlie Brown confides to Lucy that, when he grows up, he wants to marry someone who will call him "Poor, sweet baby." Lucy, of course, thinks this is really stupid, but Snoopy comes over and licks his face while thinking, "Poor, sweet baby."

Okay, it loses something in the translation, but it's funny to us. That's how I looked at our marriage too! A lot of it may have been based in my *nature,* but my *nurture* can take its share of the credit. My mother had more **S** than almost anyone I've ever known. Cindy says Mom made Mother Teresa look like a hitman for the Mob! She was reared in a male-dominated home in which "the boys" usually got their way. Combine her *nature* (**S**) with her *nurture,* and you will understand why she so often deferred to me, The Crown Prince, as I grew up. (This term is not how I referred to myself, but my twin sister, Ellen, would say I charmed my way through school, while she studied and worked her way through.)

I grew up seldom having to do what I disliked—not really spoiled, but not receiving hard lessons of discipline that would have helped me grow up sooner. I became very skilled at talking my way *out of* trouble and *into* having my own way. I was accustomed to being appeased and coddled. The first time after our wedding that I had a bad headache, I told Cindy I was really in pain. She responded, "What have you taken for it?" I said, "Nothing." And she replied, "Well...?"

That's why Charlie Brown makes us laugh. What I *expected* from her was, "Poor, sweet baby," and what I got was more like, "Dummy, take an aspirin!"

In case you haven't figured it out, God did not bless Cindy with naturally overflowing **S** traits. Instead, she has been blessed with what I need to balance out what was lacking in my style and my upbringing. I am thankful daily for her character and contributions, even though I was not grateful at the time. Our wedding vows included a line about *completing* rather than *competing*, even though we didn't understand how *competing* pulled us apart and *completing* brought us together, as shown below.

For much of my life, I looked for "Poor, sweet baby" responses. I'm not telling you about them now because I'm proud of it. In fact, I'd rather discuss other people's histories than my own. But I know my own story better than someone else's, and I want to give you hope that your situation can also be improved as you learn and apply the personal style concepts in this book.

As another example of my immaturity in dealing with adult responsibilities, I was recruited out of The King's College in New York to road-manage a rock band. I was the youngest on the tour, working with a group of high-ego performers who had been functioning together for months *(without any help from me, thank you very much)*. I knew nothing about show business—neither the *show* part, nor the *business* part. Obviously the people who made the decision to hire me knew nothing about personal styles either.

As a result, my tour reports to the home office were always inaccurate, sloppy, and late. Daily cash intakes were in the thousands of dollars, but the money bags rolled around in my trunk for days while we desperately needed funds to keep us solvent. I was miscast as a *manager* of any sort—I couldn't manage myself.

One day, the president of the company came to straighten out the problem. He drove me around town for what seemed like hours, trying to talk some maturity and responsibility into me. I explained how *busy* I was, trying to keep everything going on the road. He said the problem wasn't that I was *busy*—I wasn't *organized*. (I remember thinking, "What's that supposed to mean?") Finally he dropped me off in front of my hotel. His last "encouraging words" were, "I haven't even seen your hotel room, but you're so *untogether,* I'll bet even your shoes aren't together. If I opened your door, it would hit one of your shoes, and the other one would be under the bed!"

As best I could, I kept my emotions together until I got to my door. I had never really *failed* at anything before in my young life. Now my charm, humor, and wit had deserted me. *People* skills don't count when you've failed in the *task* you were hired to do. I couldn't see the door lock as I fumbled with my key—my tears made it impossible. I found the lock with my thumb, guided the key into place, turned the doorknob, and the door gave way. *Klunk!* It struck one of my shoes. Of course, I found the other one under my bed.

This may sound inconsequential to you but, from that day till today, if you can *find* one of my shoes, you will always find the other one with it. Even in a small way, I knew then that I had to do something to change. I didn't know where to begin, so I began with a pair of shoes. Of course, learning about my personal style's *strengths* and *struggles* has given me power to do far more, but we all have to start somewhere.

Peter Pan grows up

One of the things Cindy liked about me early on was my emotional openness. Where others may have seen some of my behaviors as immature, she liked my ability to be spontaneous and sincere with my emotions, which are *I* type traits.

For instance, in Atlanta I once attended an after-church wedding with her, involving a couple I didn't even know. They were both divorced, in their fifties, and they were given away by their grown children, with their grandchildren watching. I got all wet-eyed, and Cindy thought that my reaction was nice, in an Alan Alda sort of way. From Atlanta, I continued on to San Francisco, and I sent her a note that said, "Having a wonderful *wish...Time* you were here!"

Do you remember how sensitive and thoughtful you were when you were *courting,* before you were *committed?* We tend to put our best selves forward when we're dating. We adapt and adjust effortlessly to each other's differences. If the Federal Trade Commission ever applied truth-in-packaging laws to dating couples, everyone would go to jail!

It's after the vows—somewhere, sometime—that the honeymoon ends and the marriage must begin. Blind love gets its eyes examined and turns up its hearing aids too. In the early years of our marriage, Cindy had to adapt and adjust far more than she should have, and she did it admirably, but my wake-up call came when our baby entered the picture. As a new mother, Cindy was no longer willing to tolerate what she had endured as a wife. It was time for Peter Pan to grow up, but I didn't know how. I didn't know what a grownup was.

At a really pivotal time, a friend asked me if I could design a cover for a new book written by his neighbor. (I had helped him with some graphics for his company, and he knew I had a creative bent.) As I read the manuscript, I was introduced to behavioral types, traits, and styles. Having written several books myself, I also recognized that the excellent content needed some polishing. Meeting with the author, I laid out my suggestions for his cover, for book illustrations, and for overall editing. "You talk a good line," is the way I remember the author's response, "but you're an *I*. You'll never finish all these things you're saying you can do for me." I reached in my briefcase and pulled out my proposed book cover, several illustrations, a corporate identity package, and the first edited chapter. He was stunned. "I knew you were going to say that," I replied. "I read your book!"

I mentioned earlier that my *I* corrects mistakes in proofreading, righting my mistakes in my mind but not on paper. So someone else has to read what I've written to make sure that I'm not just talking to myself. As Cindy read along behind me, the same thing happened to her that happened to me—*she got it!* The puzzles of her life began to fall into place, just as mine had. We had been given the new "*language*" of **DISC** to describe what was happening in our lives, and we were able to speak it, hear it, and comprehend it.

I've told you how the Personal Style Assessment Report opened our eyes to understand ourselves and others. To us, it was nothing short of a miracle and, through it, I began to bring under control some of the destructive behaviors that had plagued me for much of my life. At the same time I was starting to get the idea, Cindy was applying the information to her life too. We began to understand that the things we found most attractive about each other were the things we lacked in our own makeup. In more manageable doses, during our engagement, these traits had been different and even refreshing. Now, however, on a *daily,* married basis, our differences seemed unmanageable and unrelenting. Without a key for understanding either the origin of our behaviors or our ability to adapt and adjust from both ends of our relationship, we were frustrated with each other and our marriage most of the time. Expectations that our partner was going to fulfill the "traditional" role of husband or wife failed to recognize that neither of us ha was perfectly suited for the role. We would have to re-think our expectations, our roles, and our abilities to make adjustments. We began to see how *different* could be good and, in time, we learned to enjoy most of our differences. We began to value the contributions each of us could bring to our family.

Part of our success in appreciating our differences and adjusting our styles came because we *chose* to appreciate and adjust. It seemed like the best thing to do, so we were surprised when we met couples who used their style information as excuses to hurt each other. Several years ago, Cindy and I did 5 Monday-night seminar sessions for married couples in a nearby community. We passed out workbooks, explained the **DISC** Model of Behavior, and had everyone complete a Personal Style Questionnaire to create a graph that showed each person's *natural* style and a graph that showed each person's *adjusted* style.

Going around the room, I asked each person what they saw in their graphs and how they felt about it. I was very surprised when one woman, shaking with emotion, said, "I feel angry." Her style was very intense in both **S** and **C**. Of course, this means that stability, order, security, and predictability were keys to her sense of well-being. She pointed to her husband, whose **D** and **I** were equally intense. She continued, "Everybody loves him, but I'm the one who has to put up with him!"

Once upon a time, she found him full of boyish charm, but he never finished projects around the house that he had begun with enthusiasm. Once he tore the roof off in the middle of storm season, but didn't replace the boards and shingles until rain had destroyed her family heirlooms. Another time, he took off every door in the house to repaint them but, 2 years later, they awaited completion in the garage. She needed far more order and stability.

Whether it was because he was embarrassed and trying to keep things light in the seminar, or because he actually felt this way, his response was to shrug and reply, "What can I say? That's the way I am!"

Cindy and I feel fortunate that we decided to make our family's styles a matter for action rather than just conversation.

Chapter 16:
Style in Parenting
Relationships

Again, these personal relationship chapters intertwine, so we're not finished applying principles to marriage. In many homes, children add to the stress of adjusting as husband and wife. As the old saying goes, "Two's company; three's a crowd." Relationships between a couple become exponentially more complicated when children enter the picture. Each child has his or her own patterns, rhythms, and style right from the beginning.

Born that way

Several years ago, I met an obstetrics nurse who claimed she could often spot a newborn's basic style in the delivery room. She believed an infant's pace is easily recognized, and that many babies show a decided preference for or against people.

When our daughter, Jessica, was an infant, we knew she was awake by the sound of her cooing and singing to herself early in the morning. She "flirted" with everyone who stopped to admire her in stores. Again, we didn't know about personal styles, but we knew we had a "good baby."

When Danielle was born 3½ years later, we didn't know what to think. She didn't like being held, she didn't respond warmly to people, and we knew she was awake when we heard her fussing and grunting to herself in her crib. We still didn't know about styles, but we knew this one was a different sort of baby. She wasn't "bad," but she wasn't what we expected!

I had just assumed we would have another Jessie. Now that we understand how our children are "wired," I can explain their behaviors in **DISC** terms that will quickly make sense to you. Jessica has very intense *I* and *S* traits; Danielle's strongest traits seem to be *C* and *D*.

It's naturally easier for me to understand what Jessie is thinking and feeling, and it's naturally easier for Cindy to understand what's happening with Danielle. Why? Because Jessie is *naturally* more like Dad, and Danielle is *naturally* more like Mom.

Jessie's sense of humor is spontaneous and silly (*I*), while Danielle's seems more planned and amusing (*C*). Like a good *I*, Jessie is also more impressionable. When she was little, I talked her into ordering *chicken lips* at a restaurant. Danielle's response to the same tactic was to look suspiciously toward her mother and ask, "Is there such a thing?"

Danielle has always looked for things to do when she is bored. She'll go outside and throw a basketball, or she'll ride her bike. The *D* in her style wants to be *doing,* while her *C* wants to be *discovering.* She's like her mother, who has always found it difficult just to sit. Cindy often has needlework in her hands, working on a project that may take a year or two to complete.

Both of them live by lists. (Oh, I have lists too, but they

are a *coping mechanism* for me, since I tend to be distracted by many things. Danielle and Cindy make lists instinctively.) When she's bored, Danielle often goes to work on a new list. At age 7, she regularly made lists of toys, friends, names, states, foods, colors, and more. She can make a list and then reorganize it by other criteria. This

The names of the Girls Club by age

Stephanie 11
Courtney 10
Danielle 10
Bethany 8
Meg 7
Madiline 6
Haley 5

Teachers
Miss Christine
miss Cindy
miss crooks
Miss Joyce
Miss kendall

list *(right)* is of neighborhood girls who formed a club and asked her to join. You'll notice that it's arranged by age; but she might rearrange it alphabetically, or by how close the girls are to our house. The "teachers" are moms who provide activities and snacks at the weekly meetings and, of course, each girl's name and age is grouped next to her mother's name.

Our Jessie doesn't make lists. *We make lists for her!* This weekly chores chart *(right)* is an example, demonstrating that *Is* prefer approaching repetitive tasks in a fun way. There's some tongue-in-cheek humor happening here between dad and daughter that says, "Okay, Cinderella, do your duty!" Yet it tells her that doing her work with a good attitude is important. When she saw it, she laughed—and that's half the battle in working with kids who are not *task-oriented*. If *you* are *task-oriented,* you may think this approach is unnecessary. It didn't take much effort to put a light touch in Jessie's "to-do" list. We took her style's view of tasks into consideration when we made up the list.

Spoonfuls of sugar

Speaking of chores, understand that *I* and *S* types are more easily distracted from completing tasks. In her early elementary school days, Jessica's daily task was taking out the kitchen trash in the evening. She did it, but she frequently forgot to replace the trash bag in the kitchen receptacle. It was frustrating for both my wife and my daughter as, most nights, she was summoned back into the kitchen to take care of what she had left unfinished. Cindy and I knew that Jessie was not being willfully disobedient; she was being a forgetful, 8-year-old child with an *I* style. We didn't believe this was a matter of discipline or control, but of maturity. How could we get her to succeed in this task that seemed simple to us?

We looked at the obstacles in her way to do it right, and this is what we saw. She had no trouble getting the filled trash bag out of its container, or tying it up, dragging it through the kitchen door into the family room, unlocking the double doors to the patio, finding the big cans out by the shed, and coming back into the house. The problem was that, once she walked back inside and locked the outside door, her mind said, "Finito! All done!" At this point, with empty hands, she faced all kinds of distractions: a television in the family room, a little sister who might be there or calling to her from another part of the house, several directions she could walk in (only *one* leading back into the kitchen), a telephone, and a variety of other enticements.

So, one evening, I told her I would teach her how to take out the trash and always remember to replace the trash bag. I walked over, pulled the trash-filled bag from its receptacle, tied the top closed and, before walking away, glanced down and saw the *empty space* I was leaving behind. I screamed in shock and fell to the floor, clutching my heart! *Oh, no—a hole! An empty place! What could I do?*

On hands and knees, I *crawled* over to the pantry and struggled to reach the replacement bags. Then, with superhuman effort, I made my way to the container and, with my final breath, I put a new bag in place. The *crisis* had passed—our home was safe once again! Recovering from this close brush with tragedy, I regained my composure and was able, with Jessie's help, to get the trash out of the house.

Why did I go through all of this? Partly because I'm also an *I*, too, but it was a whole lot easier than letting something as easily fixed as this become a point of contention between mother and child.

Make "teachable moments" memorable

Cesare Pavese said, "We do not remember *days,* we remember *moments.*" If you can't see how memorable this event could be in the mind of an 8-year-old, you're not really trying. I know a *spanking* would also have been memorable—and it might even have cured forgetfulness—but we thought **DISC**ipline would be more effective than punishment!

We logically moved the task of *replacing* the trash bag back to coincide with the event of *removing* the bag. In the new routine, it occurred before Jessie ever left the kitchen, so she wouldn't have an opportunity to be distracted after coming back into the house. My "high drama" was just an anchor to make the task memorable. As long as we could get her to remember to *take out* the trash, we could get her to remember replacing the trash bag. Now her younger sister has this chore and does not have the same challenge.

Here's another example of making a moment memorable, and I've used it to suggest creative ways of enlisting cooperation from children. Cindy has always wished that she played piano better than she does, and we felt Jessica would enjoy being able to play a musical instrument when she becomes an adult. So we started her on piano lessons, Suzuki style, in which the mom plays along with the student, sharing the piano bench. Jessie was 9 when she started, and we felt she should take lessons for a year before deciding whether it was "her thing.". Being an *I*, she liked the idea of playing for people, but she didn't like repetitive drills on the piano. She asked if she could quit. As Cindy told her (and as *your* mother probably said to you), "If you quit this, you'll make a habit of quitting everything that's a challenge!"

There are times, as a parent, when you stop explaining why. "Because I said so!" is the best answer you can give. Our kids know better than to play one parent against another—they can't shop for a better response between Mom and Dad. Knowing that Mom's mind was made up in this matter, Jessie gave me the old "sad eyes." I got up, went to Blockbuster Video, and rented a tape of Victor Borge in one of his comedy concerts. When he fell off his piano bench and secured himself in place with a seat belt, Jessie laughed and laughed. She didn't mention quitting again that year.

I'm telling these stories as examples of adapting our *natural* teaching and parenting approach to better fit with the *natural* learning style of a specific child.

Good cop, bad cop

A family's approach to discipline is sometimes a source of disagreement in the parents' relationship. Because of their style, some parents emphasize *control,* while others emphasize *self-expression.* Some emphasize *cooperation,* while others think *compliance* is the key.

As someone with strong *D* and *C,* Cindy has said that she sometimes feels like she has to play Attila the Hun, while I get to come off as Goodtime Charlie, using my *I* and *S.* If so, this is an unfair role for her. After all, she's our family's activity planner and outings instigator, and the founder and keeper of family traditions.

Employees in some of my businesses have said that I can even make a turndown "NO" sound positive. It's a function of my style. However, if this means I get to play the "good cop" in our parenting partnership, and Cindy is cast as the "bad cop," both of us get short-changed, and we don't provide a good model for our children either.

It is *naturally* easier for me to give in—I've got more natural *S* in my style than Cindy. It's *naturally* easier for her to seek compliance—she has more *C.* But it is vital for us to stick together as parents, rather than fighting over style differences with our kids as the battlefield. I have told them, "One day, you'll be grown and gone but, God willing, Mom and I will have many more years of us. So, as much as I love you, my first commitment is to her. Never try to get between us."

Which side of the discipline/permissiveness fence do you find yourself on? Understanding your personal style helps you know "which way you tilt." It is easier for someone with a huge to-do list (like Cindy) to say "No" to childish requests. But, in spite of her schedule, she makes time for fun.

For my part, I understand that I'd rather say "Yes," or even "Not now," than "No." But my kids can't get the idea that I'm a pushover or easily manipulated. So a "No" from either parent is a "No" from both. It's a solid relationship.

Recently, one of our daughters asked me for permission to do something, and I said "No." It wasn't all that important. It wouldn't have killed me to say "Yes," but I declined. She handled it in typical stride, saying "Okay" and walking away to do something else. I called her back and asked, "Do you know why I said No?" She shook her head. I replied, "Because I want you to know that I remember how." She smiled back at me. "You can't always get a Yes out of me when you ask. I may say No just to stay in practice." As a parent, I have a responsibility to choose what is best for my child.

If you're a "yes man," this may make sense to you. If not, you may think I've lost my mind. I'm suggesting that, as parents, we can move outside of our boxes a little bit. Whether "Yes" or "No" is more comfortable, natural, or predictable for you, try a different answer once in a while!

Bob, one of our church's pastors, is completing his PhD in counseling and does a lot of family-related teaching. Once, their older daughter complained that her younger sister got to do things that she was never allowed to do. Older siblings often complain that parents were more strict with them than with younger siblings, but his daughter wasn't saying that. Rather, her younger sister had more freedom and choices *now*.

Hearing this, I jumped to the conclusion that the younger daughter had shown wisdom and discretion repeatedly, while the older daughter had demonstrated poor judgment. Bob's explanation was very different from what I expected. He told their older daughter that she was so quiet about her life that he didn't know what she was thinking. Therefore, he and his wife felt a need to be more guarded about granting new freedoms. On the other hand, her younger sister was more open to sharing what was on her mind, so the parents knew what they could expect in her attitudes and behavior.

It's easier for us to "read" Jessie than Danielle, whose quiet dignity hides her feelings at times. Once, in response to Danielle's saying she had nothing to do, Cindy replied, "I'm so tired of hearing that you're *bored*." Danielle grew very quiet, and only as we saw shadows under her eyes did we know she was upset. I asked, "Danielle, what's wrong?" That unleashed a flood of emotion as she collapsed in a heap, sobbing, "Mommy said she's tired that I was *born!*" Of course, Cindy scooped her up and explained what she had really said. Danielle recovered her composure after a few minutes of being hugged and reassured, but she would have stoically carried her enormous hurt inside if we hadn't noticed something was wrong.

On the following 2 pages are 4 charts that provide some valuable insights and suggestions for parenting according to your style's strengths and what your child's style needs.

If your child is a: **Make sure to...**

D
- Provide your child with choices whenever possible.
- Avoid arguing or threatening.
- Allow some opportunities for personal control.
- Set and enforce limits.
- Avoid power plays and power struggles.

I
- Find ways to have fun when working with your child.
- Model firm resistance to peer pressure.
- Provide clear, simple—even written—instructions.
- Avoid withholding praise or acceptance as discipline.
- Listen, and encourage development of verbal skills.

S
- Be extra careful of hurtful words and tone-of-voice.
- Encourage, but do not force, decision-making.
- Avoid expecting or compelling individual competitiveness.
- Reassure often, and schedule personal time.
- Avoid unfavorable comparisons to others.

C
- Provide time for deciding and adjusting to change.
- Teach that perfection is not required for success.
- Allow opportunities to discover their own mistakes.
- Provide quality answers to their involved questions.
- Recognize and praise practical problem-solving skills.

If your child is a: **Make sure to...**

D
- Enforce predefined limits with predetermined discipline.
- Avoid backing away from challenges or confrontations.
- Be consistent, and avoid allowing for "wiggle room."
- Be brief and specific in giving guidance and correction.
- Guard your reserves; maintain control of the situation.

I
- Recognize your tendency to be overly lenient.
- Teach consequences rather than rescuing your child.
- Listen as much as you talk—don't be overly distracted.
- Demonstrate control over your own impulsiveness.
- Be specific in writing out assignments and to-do lists.

S
- Slow your pace, while teaching them adaptability.
- Show sincere appreciation in your comments.
- Provide advance warning of upcoming changes.
- Correct and praise privately—praise more.
- Allow time for learning to make confident decisions.

C
- Be specific, rather than general, in your praise.
- Control your own impulsiveness; expect caution.
- Choose your words carefully when making corrections.
- Listen carefully to the meaning behind comments.
- Provide for your child to have quiet time, alone.

If your child is a: **Make sure to...**

D
- Allow some control without being controlled.
- Recognize their desire for some independence.
- Expect and prepare to meet challenge.
- Be consistent and firm on matters of principle.
- Win decisively, if you must win—without guilt.

I
- Don't enable irresponsibility by rescuing them.
- Write down step-by-step instructions, in duplicate.
- Instill organizational habits by repeated practice.
- Recognize "smooth talk" and require details.
- Be careful about giving permission without limits.

S
- Avoid sheltering your child from healthy conflict.
- Teach them how to vocalize hurts and attitudes.
- Help them gain confidence in making decisions.
- Find opportunities for their independent success.
- Encourage them to read "people skill" books.

C
- Honor their need for privacy and dignity.
- Understand their controlled, less emotional responses.
- Find what is praiseworthy, but don't flatter them.
- Provide time for recharging without interruption.
- Demonstrate self-acceptance and tolerance.

If your child is a: **Make sure to...**

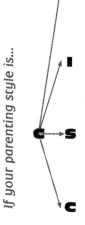

D
- Avoid "improving" their projects or accomplishments.
- Help them understand wise limits in taking risks.
- Understand their need to "go and do."
- Establish reasonable, achievable standards.
- Praise their ability to set and reach goals.

I
- Avoid bogging down in details they won't understand.
- Commend accomplishments and strengths often.
- Approve of improvement; don't expect perfection.
- Make time for laughter, activity, fun and spontaneity.
- Listen to their stories without dismissing them.

S
- Learn to articulate your feelings more warmly.
- Provide detailed explanations for tasks.
- Be especially tactful in offering suggestions.
- Gently teach some of your critical-thinking skills.
- Show acceptance, and praise whatever is worthy.

C
- Accept their suggestions and improvements.
- Correct gently and tactfully, as you wish others would.
- Recognize your mutual need to express affection.
- Show them how to set and reach reasonable standards.
- Listen to their criticism without becoming critical.

Teach the children well

Much of parenting is providing *individual* care and guidance. It can't be accomplished with a cookie-cutter approach, but it is beneficial to gain insights by listening to other parents' experiences and relating them to your child's style.

Any parents exposed to religious training have heard Proverbs 22:6, which says, "Train a child in the way he should go, and when he is old he will not turn from it."

The Book of Proverbs (also known as Wisdom) provides practical insights for living, but problems arise if we misunderstand what it says and attempt to apply our own meaning. For instance, regardless of what you may have heard from others, this Proverb does not say that, if we bring our kids up right, they will stay out of trouble as they get older. The phrase "in the way he should go" is better translated from the Hebrew, "according to his way"—his *derek,* meaning his inner direction or bent. In *Different Children, Different Needs,* Dr. Charles F. Boyd, renders the verse this way: "Adapt the training of your child so that it is in keeping with his natural design; when he comes to maturity, he will not depart from that pattern of life."

In other words, Charlie says, "Nurture your children according to their nature." *We can write what has not yet been written on their hearts.* However, babies do not come to us as "blank slates," ready to have written on them whatever a parent wishes. They arrive with some scripting already written on their slates for them.

This leads me to tell you that there is more to understanding your style (and your child's) than just identifying a particular pattern of behavior and giving it a label. Just as we are more than simply *D, I, S,* or *C* (each of us is a blend of all 4 types in varying intensities), we are also more than the sum of these traits. In addition to observable *behaviors,* we also have *thinking* styles, *detail* styles, *values,* and more. **DISC** is readily observed and understood, but it is not intended to answer every question about people. Discovering your child's inner wiring—his or her *bent*—is a process. Still, I think **DISC** is the best place to begin in building a healthy, lifelong relationship with your child.

When I deliver talks or workshops about personal styles, people often tell me they feel cheated. "Why didn't anyone tell me about this when I was growing up? Why wasn't I taught this in school? Think where I would be if I had known then...."

If you're a parent, you may be wondering when it is appropriate to introduce your children to their personal styles. We were beginning to discover **DISC** when our older daughter was 7, and she heard us talking about the ideas. As we drove around town, we played a few cassette tapes that explained the concept. I was in a new job developing **DISC**-related products and seminars, and I had a learning curve to conquer. So our kids just grew up around it. You can imagine our surprise when friends told us how Jessie, then 8, had explained the whole concept to them as she rode to their house one Sunday after church to play with their kids!

Our children's understanding of style issues has made our lives easier. There are times when Cindy's to-do list is longer than the hours available to accomplish the tasks. When she tells our girls, "Today is a *High D* day!", they know she means that everyone needs to "pick up the pace, stay on task, and get it done." They don't wonder if Mom is angry or upset;

they know it's just time for serious "go and do." One afternoon, they returned from such a day and reported, "Mom was driving in '**D** *gear*' all day! She got behind this pokey driver, and she said, 'You've got a pretty sad life when the *best* you can do with it is the speed limit!'"

Once, early on, Jessie was being corrected for something she had neglected, and she said, "I just wish I wasn't an *I*." We quickly made it clear that her personal style was never an easy excuse for a mistake. This was when we first began talking about *strengths* and *struggles*—that we all have areas where we can improve, but that we can't fault our style as a way to avoid responsibility for our actions and attitudes.

Provide a reason to grow

I'm not trying to turn this chapter into a hymn of praise to my children (*fat chance you'll believe that!*), but they've been with us long enough that I have a million stories about them. Here's another:

A few years ago, we were concerned about Jessie's increasing shyness. Her *I* traits are accompanied by similarly intense *S* traits, and some of the things we "knew" she would enjoy were being missed. We thought she was lacking in initiative. We discussed her shyness on several occasions, not pushing her, but encouraging her to venture outside her "*S-stands-for-shy*" comfort zone a little more.

One Thanksgiving evening, we were eating dinner at the *Omni Rosen* hotel in Orlando. The next morning, we would be setting up for some **DISC**-based seminars, and we were enjoying a gourmet holiday meal. We heard a familiar, scratchy voice in the almost-empty dining room and realized that we were 2 tables away from Mickey Rooney. Danielle was too young to know him, but Jessie recognized him from *The Black Stallion, Pete's Dragon,* and his black-and-white movies on cable television. And she wanted his autograph! She felt too shy to ask, but how could she receive without asking? Because her new goal was strong enough, she took a risk and tried something uncomfortable.

Waiting for a lull in his table conversation, she approached him and, in front of his dinner guests, said, "I'm sorry to interrupt, but my name is Jessica, and I'm from Atlanta. We were at Disney World all day today, and I never saw Mickey Mouse once. But that's okay, because *you're* the *real* Mickey, anyway! Could I have your autograph, please?" You could hear the *"ooohs"* and *"ahhhhs"* all over the room—*what a wonderful little girl you are!* Of course, she still treasures the autograph, and we treasure the risk Jessie took to conquer her shyness.

What gave Jessie courage to change? The same thing that gave her father the courage to begin growing up. The same thing that will give you and your children courage to tackle some of the style *struggles* in life: when the pain of staying where we are becomes greater than the risk of moving ahead, we'll be willing to change. Or, to state it from a more positive view, "When your dream is big enough, the 'facts' don't count!" People need reasons to change for the better.

It's like the old hound dog that was lying on the porch of a country cabin. Once in a while, the dog would raise his head, howl loudly, and then flop his head back down on the floor. Someone asked the dog's owner, "What's wrong with your dawg?" The owner replied, "He's layin' on a nail."

"Well, why don't he move?"

"It don't hurt enough to move," said the owner, "just enough to complain about it."

Parents can't *make* style adjustments happen in their children but, by being aware of key *struggles* early, parents can build an atmosphere of encouragement and incentive to make it less risky as children venture out into new territory.

"Poor, sweet baby" is not a response that encourages growth and change, either in adults or in children. Sometimes, as parents, we even have to be a nail. That doesn't mean we have to be cruel or overly critical in correcting our children. It means that we can find style-appropriate ways to build dreams in them that scare away both their unspoken fears and the supposed facts that are holding them back. Being an influence for growth in our children means finding ways to encourage and inspire them as often as we correct and discipline them.

Many positive suggestions are available in *Different Children, Different Needs.* While you're picking up that book, also look for *Children Are Wet Cement* (Old Tappan, NJ; Fleming H. Revell Co., 1995) by Anne Ortlund. While not written from the perspective of behavioral types, this book contains a wealth of helpful ideas, written in an approach that will appeal to your personal style.

Helping children learn

There is more to the way children learn that their personal styles, but parents would be wise to include styles as a major factor in the school experience. Children who do especially well in school are often those whose style fits the environment. Knowing what you now know about styles, place check marks in the boxes below, to identify those students who most *naturally* perform successfully within these parameters.

	D	I	S	C
• Sit quietly for lengthy periods?	☐	☐	☐	☐
• Raise hands to speak?	☐	☐	☐	☐
• Wait for their turn?	☐	☐	☐	☐
• Pay attention?	☐	☐	☐	☐
• Take notes?	☐	☐	☐	☐
• Organize / synthesize concepts?	☐	☐	☐	☐
• Follow written instructions?	☐	☐	☐	☐
• Speak and act respectfully?	☐	☐	☐	☐
• Submit to authority?	☐	☐	☐	☐
• Demonstrate patience?	☐	☐	☐	☐
• Complete home assignments?	☐	☐	☐	☐
• Work well in teams?	☐	☐	☐	☐

No surprises here! Students who do well under this structure tend to have *slower-paced, reserved, introverted* styles. Of course, *fast-paced, outgoing, extroverted* styles can succeed at school, but you can see that, for many **D** and **I** type children, this can be a hostile environment!

Several years ago, I had opportunities to participate with classroom teachers in week-long training conferences sponsored by the state's private school association. It is important to note that these were *private-school* teachers, because we tend to think of their pupils as being "better" students who have been screened for disruptive behavior or discipline problems.

Still, after the **DISC** training, almost every teacher voiced a wish that this information had been available to them in college. One of their course assignments was to describe an actual classroom scenario and how they would have handled it differently if they had understood their own style and the styles of others involved. Almost every participant, from kindergarten teachers to high school coaches, envisioned more successful interactions and happier outcomes if they had known how to apply **DISC** to their situation.

If you have a child (or a *student!*) who is not fitting well into the classroom environment, consider sharing the **DISC** information. Children should understand their personal styles, and so should teachers. Sometimes it's easier to label an unchallenged student as "disruptive," or a restless student as "hyperactive" than to deal wisely with them. Styles should never be used to excuse misbehavior or shirking of responsibilities, but this information may resolve common classroom challenges.

Finally, many parents worry about safety in schools. Teaching children how to negotiate and resolve conflict is a lifetime skill, and sometimes a *life-saving* skill, in our increasingly edgy society. If students understood that people do things *for themselves*, rather than *against us* (as Charles Boyd often says), we would see a reduction in bullying, hostility, and aggression. By appreciating, honoring, and using their differences, they would learn how to open doors to success throughout their lives.

Chapter 17:
Style in
Friendships

Ralph Waldo Emerson wrote, "We take care of our health, we lay up money, we make our roof tight and our clothing sufficient, but who provides wisely that he shall not be wanting in the best property of all—friends?" This is the focus for this final chapter on *personal* relationships.

This is not intended as a warm and fuzzy tribute to the necessity of having "huggers" in your life. Friendship is more than that and, to some of us, nothing like that at all! The 4 different types view the state and the act of friendship in different ways, and identifying those is a good way to begin.

D type friendships

To most **D** type individuals, friendship is rough-and-tumble, give-and-take. Remember, these are people who speak their mind, so those who are easily offended or fearful of a frank, open exchange seldom venture close. Preferring to keep short accounts, they cut to the bottom line, tell you what they think, and move on. They tend not to hold grudges, while those who have experienced their direct, frontal assault, are still licking their wounds. Often, the spouse of a **D** type individual has the opposite characteristics. I have met many such couples who make a dynamic team. It's as if one does the cutting, and the other comes along right behind to put on the bandage! Likewise, I have seen friendships, and even business partnerships, that operate in the same manner. This is the basic formula for "good cop–bad cop," as referenced earlier.

David Grayson's comment reflects a **D**'s concept of true friendship: "No real friendship is ever made without an initial clashing which discloses the metal of each to each."

What a wonderful thing it can be to have a **D** type friend who naturally moves to your defense. An offense against you is an affront against them! Sometimes they are more ready to *join* the fight to protect you than you are ready to *start* the fight. Expect your authenticity to be challenged in beginning a relationship with those who have lots of **D** in their style. As noted in Grayson's remark, they want to know what you're made of. Is your true nature *fight* or *flight*?

Before Cindy and I were married, we had dinner in St. Petersburg, Florida, with the man who had made the comment years before about my shoes not being together. By this time, I had progressed enough that he and I had become good friends. Both he and my future wife have lots of **D** in their styles and, in their first meeting, he seemed to be pushing and probing. Not understanding the dynamics of their conversation, I was amazed—and almost aghast! As he conducted his inquisition, Cindy, unfazed, replied, "I have a feeling I should have brought a résumé."

It seemed to me like a stare-down, and the first one to blink would be the loser. My friend replied, "Well, these are questions you wouldn't ask a friend. We really don't know each other yet and, when we do, I'm sure we'll be friends. But I've got a lot invested in this guy [me], and I'd like to know what you're about." One of the things he liked very much about Cindy was her ability to "take it."

Other styles may not react to the **D**'s confrontational pattern as well. For instance, 2 brothers had a lot of rough-and-tumble conflict growing up. Jeff, the older, has lots of **D**, while Steve, the younger, has lots of **S**. When Jeff got upset with Steve, he would confront the problem directly—and physically! Several minutes later, he would ask Steve to go outside and play ball with him. Steve, still nursing his wounds, would respond, "Play with you? You *hit* me! I never want to see you again!" To big brother Jeff, it was "nothing personal" when he was "pounding on" little brother Steve. To Steve, it was *only personal* to be pounded on. Years later, as adults, they no longer resolve their disagreements in this manner. Jeff has matured, and Steve is a champion kick-boxer!

When **D** type individuals make decisions about tasks and goals, they often disassociate the personal issues involved. They can see their decisions and actions as "nothing personal—just business." Because they have this ability, they expect others to understand. Both sides in such relationships need to understand the view of the other. Recall our "oven mitt" analogy on Page 102 to avoid burning or being burned.

Sometimes kids work out such differences very honestly. I was discussing 2 teenagers from our church with one of their mothers, telling her that I was amazed by how well her son gets along with this friend, since they are polar opposites in their styles. Thomas has a very *active* blend of **D** and **I** traits, while David has a very *passive* blend of **S** and **C** traits. She said that they usually get along well for a day or so in close contact, although sometimes, it doesn't take much time for them to wear on each other. When that point arrives, one of them announces that he needs some breathing room and goes home. In a day or so, their energies are recharged and they are ready to get together again.

If friendship with another person is strained because of the differences in your styles, it's all right to put some distance between you at times. But note that, for these teenagers, the separation is by mutual agreement and without rejecting the other person. Sounds insightful and mature, doesn't it?

I type friendships

To most *I* type individuals, there are no strangers—just friends they haven't met. Remember, these are trusting people who view the world as an exciting place with new adventures around every corner, and they are readily available to everyone they meet. Usually, others must prove themselves to be unworthy of an *I*'s trust.

It's interesting to see how often their spouses are opposite in style. Many times, I have said that Cindy's style is a real complement to my style. If someone has doubts about my legitimacy, they meet her and immediately decide there must be something about me they have overlooked.

Several people have told me this was true of Roy and Walt Disney as well. (Yes, I know they were brothers, but this story fits well in a section about friends.) Walt was a creative genius, but was not very successful in handling his money.

He had gone through several bankruptcies, and none of his potential investors was confident about his ability to make his Disneyland idea into a reality. (Art Linkletter said that, for every step he took in and out of the Anaheim orange grove that was to become Disneyland, he lost a million dollars, because he decided not to fund Walt's idea.) When Roy Disney came on board, he was able to attract investors quickly. He brought credibility that transferred to Walt and his dream.

For *Is*, the *quantity* of their friendships is as important as the *quality*, and they tend to be much less discriminating when allowing people into their "inner circle." Our daughter, Danielle, used to attend second grade with a great little boy named Sam. Parents took turns car-pooling to classes. One day, Sam was riding along with us. He knew my wife and daughters well, but didn't know me at all. I enjoyed listening to his exclamation-pointed conversation, bringing us up to date on his latest exploits. At one point, when he said, "And then, my best friend, David...," I interrupted him. "Sam," I blurted, "I thought *I* was your best friend!" He replied, "You are, but my *other* best friend, David...." This was a sure sign that we were dealing with an *I*. Everyone was, at least potentially, Sam's best friend.

This instant embrace is surprising to many, but *Is* respond instinctively in this manner. They are surprised when the rest of the world does not react similarly. I saw this in action recently when I was out for a walk. I passed a man who was working in a front yard several blocks away from our house. He had been measuring from the curb to a spot several yards up into the yard. He had measured to the same spot from the front of the house. Obviously, he was trying to establish a marker for something. By the time I reached him, he was measuring across the width of the yard, having secured one end of his tape measure on the blade of his shovel. I didn't know if he was a landscaper or the homeowner so, as I passed, I called out to him, "Digging up or putting back?" He replied, "Putting *what* back?" I was stunned. *How could he be so thick-headed?* I shouted back, "I mean, what are you doing?" He replied with one word: "Bushes."

I mentioned this to Jessie and asked her, "If I saw you measuring and you had a shovel, and if I asked if you were 'digging up or putting back,' what would you think I meant?" She said, "You'd want to know what I was doing. It was an invitation to talk." But the man wasn't interested in talking or in deciphering my meaning. He wanted to complete his task, and if I meant, "What are you doing in the lawn that requires measurement?," I should have asked!

As I continued my walk, a car began to pass me. (Our subdivision has no sidewalks, so, as I walk at the edge of the road, I often wave at passing drivers to say thanks for not turning me into roadkill.) This driver looked at me, but never removed his hands from the "ten and two" position on his steering wheel. He did not lift a finger in acknowledgment; he did not crack a smile or raise an eyebrow in recognition; he drove by. My immediate thought was *everybody's weird today—first the digger and now the driver!* Two folks were focused on tasks, and my day was going downhill. No one was glad to see me! I didn't feel like waving at the next car that passed me, but I did. It was driven by a lady who waved back enthusiastically and smiled as she mouthed a friendly, "Hello!" *I* type behavior oozed out of this stranger, and I suddenly felt the neighborhood was friendly again.

*I*s prefer to be around people who are not too serious and contemplative. In his diaries, Evelyn Waugh wrote, "We cherish our friends not for their ability to amuse us, but for ours to amuse them." When *I*s are in a less fun environment, they work to change it, to bring up the energy and tempo, or to get people laughing and enjoying the humor they inject into the situation.

I found myself doing this in a telephone conversation with a prospective client. He was so reserved in his responses that I found myself being a little goofy, just trying to generate a lighter tone. (This is not a recommended approach when trying to convince a **C** that you are the authoritative consultant he needs!) When it was time to meet with him, I brought along my vice president, Rick, who also has a lot of **C**. I wanted someone there on *my* team who could help me avoid repeating the same behavior.

In effect, I recognized that I was in danger of setting off firecrackers at the wrong time, recalling our *I* analogy on Page 103. Remember, under stress, *I*s tend to look for ways to introduce levity. Having Rick along provided me with a measure of self-protection. I felt more self-assured and focused, knowing that these 2 men had similar styles, and that Rick's influence would help me be appropriate in my conduct.

I could have saved this story for the upcoming *professional* relationships portion, but I have mentioned it here for 2 reasons. Rick proved himself a faithful friend before he was a business partner, so I knew I could trust him to help me when the stakes were high. I also know that *you* have friends who can help you stay balanced, whatever your style's response to anxiety.

A number of years ago, my friend, Hal, who has mostly **C** traits, asked me a question that has deeply impacted my life. "If I saw something in your life that was holding you back, would you want me to tell you about it?" Hal isn't a pushy man who confronts lightly or easily. He has been a great source of encouragement to me in my struggles. He was asking permission to help me grow. The great thing about the way he asked was that I knew saying, "No, I'm not ready for that," would not have *damaged* our relationship. I knew, however, that saying, "Yes, I will trust you," was the way to *deepen* it.

Being the friend of someone with a lot of **I** requires emotional stamina because of their impulsiveness, but it's good to know someone who always looks for the bright side of life.

S type friendships

To be numbered among the true friends of an **S** type person is an honor. They value *quality* over *quantity* and, in relationships, they tend to give even more than they receive. They are loyal and thoughtful, often looking for small ways to show care and interest. It is natural for many of them to remember details about your family and things you have expressed concern over, and then to ask you about them with genuine interest.

A quotation that well describes their view of friendship comes from Aristotle: "Friends are an aid to the young, to guard them from error; to the elderly, to attend to their wants and to supplement their failing power of action; to those in the prime of life, to assist them to noble deeds."

My friend, Richard, is generous to a fault. One of his businesses is discovering and providing positive, worthwhile books to entrepreneurs and small business owners. When our kids were little, Richard often gave Cindy or me a book he thought would benefit the girls. If he had something that would help me, he would grab it off his book display and put it into my hands, even when he knew I didn't have the money to pay for it. "If it helps you, we'll straighten it out later," was his usual statement.

Once, our family attended a business convention in Louisville, Kentucky, where Richard had a book table. When he found out that his hotel suite was larger than our room, he offered to switch with us.

A freak blizzard hit the city just as we were leaving, and we couldn't drive our car home, so we got a ride back to Atlanta with friends who were better prepared for bad weather. The following weekend, I flew back to Louisville with a friend who also had to pick up his car. We were told that the hotel was sold out, and my friend wondered aloud if we could get away with "crashing" overnight on a couch in the lobby. "No," I said, "but Richard is at this convention too. Let's go find him."

When we located Richard's book display, he quickly agreed to share his hotel suite and handed me the key. Then he asked if we had eaten yet. He handed us an unopened 2-liter bottle of Coke and a large, warm pizza. He said it was an "extra." Not only is Richard generous, but he is compulsively so. By the time he had walked us to the lobby, he had offered "our" pizza, slice-by-slice, to several other friends as well!

We have laughed together about this on several occasions. True to his style, Richard is always a loyal friend, encourager, and giver.

People with an *S* style build close relationships slowly. They do not reveal their emotions or feelings carelessly, while *I*s emote their way through life. A number of years ago, I was very surprised when a good friend in St. Louis seemed less excited to see me than I was to see her. Because I have overwhelming *I* in my personal style, I tend to pick up relationships right where I left them, even if several years have passed. But *S*s are not like microwave ovens—they don't warm up quickly. Although we were all good friends, she shared with my wife that she hadn't heard from me in quite a while, and she needed time to adjust to a feeling that she wasn't important enough to be remembered between visits.

William James observed, "Human beings are born into this little span of life, of which the best thing is its friendships and intimacies...and yet they leave their friendships and intimacies with no cultivation, to grow as they will by the roadside, expecting them to 'keep' by force of inertia." For *S* type individuals, this is innate knowledge. For the rest of us, this truth must be learned.

Ralph Waldo Emerson wrote, "Go oft to the house of thy friend, for weeds choke the unused path." Remember that Emerson addressed the verb "go" to you. Do not expect your *S* friend to take the initiative in coming to you. And, given their dislike of surprises, I'm not suggesting that unscheduled visits are the best way to pursue their friendship. But when you think to call them and invite them to participate in your life and friendship, you demonstrate loyalty and thoughtfulness.

Do you remember how you met your **S** friend? I have spoken to people who don't remember the specific event because there was no magical, memorable moment in the meeting. It just seems that this person has always been their friend. **S** type people don't often call attention to themselves, although they may remember better how *they* met *you.*

Cindy and I attended a National Speakers Association (NSA) dinner for new members. We enjoy attending these get-togethers because of the camaraderie and great food. Our friend, Mike, is a gourmet chef and speaker/trainer who always puts together an amazing menu and feeds 50–75 of us. Just a few minutes ago, I was thinking of a great **S** example involving Mike when the telephone rang. It was Mike just calling to thank us for attending and to thank Cindy, especially, for helping to clean the kitchen afterwards. *Appreciation* is a major factor in the values of **S** type people, and they are usually quick to express their own thanks.

My *real* story about Mike goes back to Christmastime, when he approached me at the NSA meeting with a small plastic bag filled with an amazing concoction of spices. He explained that this was his secret recipe for hot apple cider, and he hoped our family would enjoy it during the holidays. I said thanks and brought it home. After New Year's Day, I sent this e-mail to Mike expressing how much we enjoyed it:

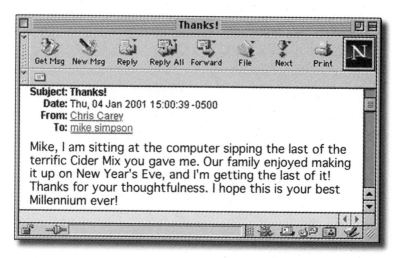

Thanks!

Get Msg   New Msg   Reply   Reply All   Forward   File   Next   Print

Subject: Thanks!
    Date: Thu, 04 Jan 2001 15:00:39 -0500
  From: Chris Carey
     To: mike simpson

Mike, I am sitting at the computer sipping the last of the terrific Cider Mix you gave me. Our family enjoyed making it up on New Year's Eve, and I'm getting the last of it! Thanks for your thoughtfulness. I hope this is your best Millennium ever!

Later that month at the NSA meeting, Mike enthusiastically thanked me for sending him the note. He said that it meant a lot to him. He had given out more than a hundred bags of the mix to friends before Christmas but, in the hustle of the holidays, just a handful of folks had sent him a note, or called him, to say they had enjoyed it. Was Mike complaining? Not at all. He didn't do it for gushy thanks. He did it to add something special to the season. Being told that it was appreciated had just made him feel good, and he was expressing that thought. This is the moral of the story: **S** type people appreciate thoughtful, little gestures, and they love it when others appreciate their thoughtfulness too.

One modern translation of the Book of Proverbs contains this wisdom: "A man that hath friends must show himself friendly" (*Proverbs 18:24*). To *have* a friend, *be* a friend. Another translation says that we should understand that a true friend is not behind every friendly face. I am thankful for my steady **S** type friends.

C type friendships

Most **C** type individuals acknowledge friendships as necessary components in a balanced life. Because they are introverted and cautious about risk, they tend to be as methodical and careful about relationships as they are about all other areas of living. Many are very curious, fascinated by their observations of family members, coworkers, and acquaintances. They may ask probing questions, designed to draw out the *how* and *why* of others' behavior.

Sometimes these tendencies combine to make **C**s seem aloof, as if they would rather stand at a distance and watch than participate. In part, this is true, but they are both capable and desirous of long-term, high-quality, committed relationships. Statistically, their most harmonious alliances are with those of similar style with whom they can agree on priorities, methods, and procedures.

Cs are usually modest. They don't "toot their own horn" or engage in rivalries, because they live according to their own standards, which are often higher and stricter than what is generally expected. Not "chatty," their conversations tend to be logical and directed toward a purpose.

Spontaneity is not a part of their day-to-day life. Florence Littauer, who has written several books about behavioral styles, including *Personality Plus* (Old Tappan, NJ; Fleming H. Revell Company, 1992), loves to tell stories about her marriage to her husband, Fred, who has lots of **C** in his style. Florence is very spontaneous and exhibits *I* and *D* traits. She says, shortly after their marriage, he watched her eating from a cluster of grapes and was appalled that she didn't have a nail clipper to remove just several grapes at a time, neatly retaining symmetry in the bunch. She didn't believe anyone actually thought that way until he produced his nail clipper and showed her the "correct" way to eat grapes. Another time, she says, she asked him to stop for an ice cream cone, but he wouldn't because it wasn't on the day's to-do list. He said that, the next time she thought she was going to be spontaneous, she should tell him several days in advance so he could plan ahead for it!

I don't know of another **C** type individual who is this finicky, but people with this style like it when things are neat and tidy and schedules are running smoothly. A fictional hyper-**C** is Felix Unger, the fastidious roommate who drove Oscar Madison (a fictional hyper-**D**) to frustration in *The Odd Couple*. Of course, Oscar's behavior was as much a puzzle to Felix!

These kinds of mismatches lead to irritation unless the individuals involved learn how to adapt and adjust to each other for the sake of the relationship or for a higher cause. Several years ago, I heard that the way picky details are addressed is the major reason missionary workers drop out of service and return home. Think about all of the adjustments missionaries make. They must often learn a new language, and the local customs and preferences may be very different from home. Lives of patient self-sacrifice are expected. When the few remaining creature comforts are endangered because another missionary squeezes the toothpaste tube at the middle, rather than rolling it up from the bottom, or when bathroom tissue is put on the roller upside down, it can be the unforgivable difference that "proves" that these individuals can *never* work together as a team! Again, when we are under stress, we tend to lose some of our resilience and ability to stretch and adjust. Sometimes it's a *specific decision of our will* to adapt to *optional* changes when we're *forced* to change in other areas.

For this reason, **C**s tend to be more drawn to people with similar styles. George Washington once advised, "Be courteous to all, but intimate with few, and let those few be well tried before you give them your confidence." In practical terms, this means that, while **I**s and **S**s may willingly follow a **D** type leader because of his or her forceful personality, **C**s are less likely to join the parade. They place their trust cautiously, and they always know where the exits are—in case they have to get out in a hurry!

It is not true that **C**s are antisocial in their style, but they do tend to hold others to the same high level of expectations they set for themselves. Again, Washington warned, "Associate yourself with men of good quality if you esteem your own reputation, for 'tis better to be alone than in bad company."

Overfriendliness on your part causes an individual who is reserved and less emotional to question your motives. We said earlier that someone with an **S** style responds well when you say thank you for a service they have rendered. But **C**s tend to be a little suspicious if they think they are being flattered. They may wonder, "What else do they want from me?" While **I**s respond quickly to signs of emotional and physical acceptance, **C**s are wary of too much, too soon. Lord Chesterfield said, "Distrust all those who love you extremely upon a very slight acquaintance and without any viable reason."

Because they "balance the books" in every equation, Cs expect to *give* in order to *receive.*

I asked my wife for a good **C** example among our friends, and she immediately thought of another Richard, a friend of hers 10 years before I met her. He is suave, articulate, and cultured. Did I mention that he is a perfectionist? Everything he does, he does well. (We recognize this even when he fails to see it. After all, his standard is perfection.)

Several years ago, we took a family day-trip into the North Georgia Mountains, and we invited Richard and others to go with us. When he arrived at our house, he had assembled a 2-page list of interesting and worthwhile stops we could make on the way up to the mountains, if we wanted to add value to the drive. He had provided detailed directions and information about each detour and how it would enhance the experience. To us, this was a wonderful and thoughtful contribution, very appropriate from a **C**. Me? I would have just stopped at the grocery store and brought Popsicles!

Cindy also remembered a story that relates the *precise* use of the language that typifies many **C**s. Before she and I met, she commented to Richard that she felt fat and was depressed about the pounds she had added. He was horrified that she would think of herself in such terms. Convinced that his opinion was correct—and certainly more objective than her own—Richard said, "No, you are not fat. You are *Rubenesque!*"

He was, because of his interest in the fine arts, very knowledgeable about the work of the 17th Century artist, Peter Paul Rubens. In that single phrase, he totally altered

Cindy's lagging self-image and helped her see a different, beautiful perspective. Sometimes we overemphasize the criticizing eye that **C**s can focus on themselves and others but, as in this instance, their precise perspective and analysis can be far more accurate than our own. While under pressure, they can be sharp-tongued and faultfinding but, otherwise, they understand nuances and subtleties that the rest of us overlook.

Cindy and I both appreciate "our" Richard, whose **C**, under control, never neglects the refinements that distinguish the excellent from the good.

Regardless of our individual styles, you can see how each of us needs to be befriended by others. At the same time, we need to befriend others. In *Youth and Life* (Manchester, NH; Ayer Company Publishers, 1997), Randolph S. Bourne wrote, "A man with few friends is only half-developed. There are whole sides of his nature which are locked up and have never been expressed. He cannot unlock them himself. He cannot even discover them. Friends alone can stimulate him and open him."

Unfair comparisons

This is a good time to mention that *comparing one child unfavorably to another* is cheating, because one child *isn't* another! Parents do it and, unfortunately, so do teachers, relatives, friends, and others who should know better.

All of us make unfair comparisons, and not only with children. Perhaps you have a lot of **D**, or you have experience with someone who does, and you have learned that **D**s can be motivated by another's achievements. Most people, however, are demoralized by comparisons that suggest that they don't measure up to an unachievable standard.

Do spouses ever compare each other unfairly? Several years ago, we, and some of our friends and their spouses, completed style analysis questionnaires as if we were the person whom we had married. Of course, since our own style was our "norm," we were interested to see how we would score our mates' areas of *strength* and *struggle*. As it turned out, each of us scored our husband or wife lower than they really were in areas that were our own strengths. One wife, who was intensely **C**, rated her husband as an **I** with few **C** traits. Actually, his **C** traits were the highest among the 4 factors. However, she compared his style to her own, and she didn't recognize his **C** because it was no match for hers. Our own style's filters often bias our views of others. We think we are objective, even when our evaluations are highly subjective.

Sometimes when our style is out of balance, we don't recognize our behavior or others'. A high school student recently told me that his science teacher was too illogical and emotional to listen to logic. This young man's style is very much **I**, so I was amazed to hear him make this comment. Knowing the teacher well, I couldn't see anything resembling **I** in her behavior; everything about her *screams* **C** and **D**.

Because he was familiar with **DISC**, we talked in depth about the situation. His teacher believed he had violated some rules, and she had responded as might be expected of someone who is strong on *compliance*.

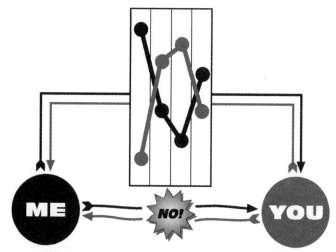

*To understand and communicate with each other, our comparisons must be with the **DISC** model, not with one another.*

In trying to explain his view to her, the student had used an emotional approach, which he mistook for logic. She was not swayed at all and quickly shot holes in his defense. Because she insisted on sticking with established rules, principles, and procedures, he thought that she was being "emotional" rather than logical. In his view, he was acting like a logical **C**, while she was acting like an irrational **I**. Because he failed to recognize his own style, his approach and interpretation were off-target. He had lost his sense of direction—like someone turned around in the woods. He first needed to identify "true North" on his "behavior compass," if he expected to find his way out.

As the above diagram shows, we should view our understanding of each other through the grids of our personal style. This will allow us to "see" many of the factors that are influencing our behavior and attitudes. We should also speak and listen in a way that communicates in the other individual's **DISC** language. When we don't take advantage of these insights, our interchange is less effective, and our meaning is often misunderstood.

In addition to comparing the actions of others with what we think we would do, especially at times when we are out of control, another unfair comparison we tend to make is with "real life" families we see on television. In *Different Children, Different Needs*, Charlie Boyd mentions growing up in the 1950s and '60s, watching shows like *Father Knows Best* and thinking that they represented "normal" life. The world is not like Andy Griffith's Mayberry, North Carolina, where we can whistle our troubles away, walking barefoot down to the lake with our fishing pole in hand. (Actually, life wasn't like that back then either!) Today's TV watchers may think that Al Bundy's household truly reflects modern, "normal" family life. Whether we imitate or excuse our family life based on television, we make a mistake. At either extreme, our unmet expectations and experiences suffer when we compare the genuine article to the standards set by its counterfeits. Comparisons are unfair.

You don't say

If you have a spouse or children, you may have heard in our story some similarities and suggestions worth applying in your own situation, but these principles will work with other family members and in other personal relationships as well. Here's a *friendship* example, dealing with communication between styles and genders.

Cindy's best friend in Atlanta—and probably in life—is a

wonderful lady named Laura. *(Actually, I met both of them together, at the same time. When I say one of them "lucked out," they both point to Laura!)* They have very little in common personality-wise, except that Cindy has **C** as one of her most *intense* traits, and Laura has **C** as her *secondary* trait. Cindy also brims with **D** and has some strong **I**, but if those were against the law, Laura's intense **S** traits would keep her safe from arrest! Still, Laura is no doormat. She has integrity, dignity, character, and courage. As friends, they complement each other wonderfully. They are known as "The Go-Places Gals."

To our daughters, "Miss Laura" is a friend and confidante who loves, accepts, and respects them. I'm out of place in this sorority of femininity, and I admire it from a respectful distance. I have noticed that men don't talk with each other the way women do. In fact, I read about a university study that reported basic differences in our conversation styles that extend beyond personal styles.

In this study, young children through adults arrived at a research facility expecting to participate in a group activity. Once there, 2 females *or* 2 males were told that there was a delay and, with only 2 folding chairs, they were sent into an empty room to wait until they were called. What occurred in that room was videotaped, as researchers studied the ways females relate to each other and the ways males relate to each other. Here's what they found:

Females arranged their folding chairs so they could look at each other while they talked. Their communication was eye-to-eye, personal, and almost leaning into each other's words. Males arranged their chairs so they would have less direct contact, and they tended to lean away from each other. Their words bounced off walls and ceilings, while their eye contact was haphazard rather than deliberate. These behaviors prevail among preschool boys and girls and continue through adulthood. Whether inborn or acquired, they are observable among "civilized" cultures.

If you and I don't know about this, and we have typical experiences with our same-sex friends, it is probable that we will expect the same level of communication to occur with our spouse, who becomes our "new best friend." The research report showed that many women thought their husbands were distant, because men don't communicate as their women friends did. Many husbands felt that their wives were intrusive, because their communication style differed from their male friends.

The study went a step further. When researchers placed couples complaining of communication difficulties in front of marriage counselors, female counselors often said that the husband was avoiding a connection, while male counselors often said that the wife's approach was smothering her husband.

This was not a study of *personal style*, but of *gender communication* differences. Knowing about it may make you more understanding of a key distinction in the ways men and women communicate. It reminds us that people don't do things *against* us, but *for* themselves. If your personal style's filters interpret these *normal patterns* as *problem signals*, you may want to reevaluate their significance.

In the interest of improving communication, I recommend your reading *The Five Love Languages : How to Express Heartfelt Commitment to Your Mate* (Chicago, IL; Northfield Pub, 1992), by Gary Chapman. This widely acclaimed book shows how we tend to give and receive love differently, according to our varying personalities. Commonly, the love languages are:

- Quality time
- Verbal communication
- Gifts
- Acts of service
- Physical touch

Sometimes we are more open to giving one type and receiving another. If we recognize these qualities in ourselves and each other, fewer misunderstandings will result, and standards can be put in place more effectively.

For instance, my love language (the way I most easily receive and understand love) involves both *verbal communication* and *touch*. (Yes, you can have more than one, and these make sense, given the intense influence of *I* in my style!) Because these are important to me, they were what I used to communicate my feelings for Cindy. She, on the other hand, is much more *task-oriented* than I, so these are not the most effective methods I could employ. If Cindy could have more of my *quality time* (a vacation that is not at all business related or tax-deductible), she would feel attended to.

Once I understood that we didn't speak the same love language, I began looking for ways to say, "What is important to you is important to me." Her other love language is *deeds of service*. I often look for a present that represents a *service* to her. For example, I know that safety and security are important to Cindy. When we check into a hotel, the first thing she does is locate the fire exits nearest our room.

She once read about a safety device called a Life Hammer, designed to break out a window if you're trapped in a submerged vehicle, and she remarked that it was a great idea, because our electric windows probably wouldn't work under water. I made a mental note. With all of her **C** qualities, she likes to be prepared for emergencies, and the Life Hammer would score extra points for me on her Love Language Meter! Last Christmas, I got excited because I thought it would be a *deed of service* if I located one and gave it to her as a stocking stuffer. However, she ordered one from a catalog and showed me how excited she was about it several weeks before Christmas. *Darn!*

In preparation for Mother's Day the following Spring, I stopped in a book store and found her the perfect present. (No, it's not a book of gooey poems about being a mom, although there would be nothing wrong with that if *verbal communication* was her love language.) *The Worst-Case Scenario Survival Handbook: Travel* (San Francisco, CA; Chronicle Books, 2001, by Joshua Piven and David Borgenicht) covers almost any emergency you could anticipate, from "How to Control a Runaway Camel" to "How to Remove a Leech." In the back, there are 12 pages attesting to the credentials and qualifications of the authors and their advisory team to write the book. This is a book that answers **C** type questions and is also a deed of service!

What do you think?

How do differing communication styles relate to personal styles? Years ago, Cindy would say to me, "I think we should...," and, when she was finished, she would ask, "What do you think?" We had a basic problem in communicating because "think" has very different meanings to a **C** and an **I**.

As a **C**, Cindy is very much a *critical thinker*. She loves weighing the pros and cons of every situation. She thinks through various options and considers the outcome. When she says, "I think...," she really means, *"I have deliberated over this carefully for some time now. I haven't mentioned it until now because I wanted to sort out the possibilities. After considering all the variables, I believe the reasonable solution is...."* It's then that she says to me, "What do you think?"

That may be what **C**-Cindy *says*, but what **I**-Chris *hears* is, *"What would you like to talk about? It's your turn now."* The cautious and correct thinker has cogitated for a while before bringing up the topic. She knows where she's headed, but the **I** has been asked for an opinion "off the top of his head." We didn't understand this for a long time, but **I** types think *out loud.*

It's not Attention Deficit Disorder, but there are a lot of ideas bouncing around in an **I**'s mind that could unsettle a **C**. For instance, if you say the word *"umbrella"* to someone with lots of **C**, they will logically think of *"rain."* If you say *"umbrella"* to someone with lots of **I**, they will just as likely think of *Mary Poppins* or *Winnie the Pooh,* both of whom carried umbrellas at one time or another. As a result of mental clutter, many *I*s "think out loud" in their attempt to separate the valuable ideas from the other "stuff." And as they talk, they gauge others' reactions and hone in on what really matters.

If *I*s are aware of this thinking pattern, it makes sense to them, but *C*s often find their ramblings unsettling. Cindy would be disturbed when I responded with something that didn't follow her line of reasoning—or sometimes even her topic.

Some *C*s might even question whether *I*s think at all. They might smugly say that *I*s "feel" rather than "think." Studies have shown that *I* and *S* types tend to rely more on *intuitive guidance* than on *logical reasoning*—something like the math whiz who can get the right answer but can't show his work to the teacher's satisfaction. I have read several research sources that claim that those who are gifted with this kind of intuition are as successful in using it to solve problems as those who use their gift of logical reasoning. On the other hand, those who possess strong intuitive skills don't do as well when they try to "logic it out." Similarly, the logical types don't do as well feeling their way through.

My point is this: Eventually, Cindy and I discovered that we filter questions differently. I tend more to *embrace* new ideas; she tends more to *evaluate* them. I am naturally optimistic about the outcome; she listens for the ticking of the time bomb. If she wants an opinion from me that makes sense to her, she knows it will take time. She'll ask and then let me think out loud. Eventually, I may even come up with a more workable solution than her own.

I have also learned that, when Cindy says, "I think...," she often means, "I have decided." I try not to treat whatever comes next as a casual thought. It's not. We have become really sophisticated in our communication. There are times now when we will tell each other, "I'm going to say this but, first, this is how I expect you to respond...." It makes thinking so much simpler!

The same is true of anyone you know in any relationship.

The ayes have it

How about decision-making between couples or friends? Styles even influence how we decide where to eat lunch. Someone with a lot of **D** traits tends to decide for everyone and figures that anyone who doesn't want to go along will speak up. Speaking up doesn't necessarily change anything but, unless challenged, a **D** is quick to decide. "Let's go here," they say. "The food is good, the service is quick, and we can get in and out quickly."

I types want everyone involved and happy, so they often try to build a consensus by coaxing and cajoling. They can be very adaptable to whatever others decide and will try to make a happy experience for everyone. "Guys, this place is really different," they say. "They have a mariachi band and piñatas—which is very unusual for a Chinese restaurant!"

S types tend to accommodate others' preferences. Generally, they won't speak up to push a personal favorite. They might find out what the majority wants to eat and recommend a place that offers that choice and options for the rest. At the least, they want to know that each person has been heard. "Whatever you want is fine," they say. "I'm not fussy."

C types sometimes make their choice according to the coupon in their purse or wallet. Eating may also be incidental to the *TASK-oriented* purpose behind their meeting. Often, they look for traditional or predictable foods, and they are, as always, cautious. "I haven't eaten here before, so if you really want sushi, let's look at the Health Inspector's certificate before we order."

You can imagine what happens when people who share a common style get ready to go out. Each *D* would be happy to make the decision. Since each might also want to drive, they could even decide to "go out together" in separate cars! Intensely *I* type adults might agree that "Chuck E. Cheese" is the place to go—food and fun in one stop! *S* types might be so intent on pleasing each other that they wouldn't decide until the restaurant had closed for the night! And *C* types might never go out, agreeing that it's better to just stay home where it's quiet and uncrowded and less expensive!

Agree to disagree

Wouldn't it be great if, as adults, we could be like the two teenage boys mentioned earlier in this chapter and choose when we associate with each other and when we've had enough? Unfortunately, the grown-up demands of work and civility don't allow this, so we have to learn to be more creative in the ways we handle style differences. (This is part of the idea behind the *oven mitt* that represents a way of relating to the *D* style. When things aren't overheated, no one needs the mitt but, when it gets too hot, knowing how to add some insulation is very helpful.)

As parents, we have become accustomed to "calling the

shots" with younger children, and we may say things, within our family, in words and tones that we would never use with our friends. Rather than always expecting those nearest to us to fit into our mold and meet our expectations, we should agree to disagree about things that are only our *preferences*, not our real *convictions*.

For example, understand that your **D** type child, like your **D** type friends, will often feel a need to be in control. Because he or she will end up controlling much in their adult lives, they can learn, from safe opportunities, to practice while growing up.

If you plainly tell a **D** type child, "Go to bed now," you may create a confrontation "opportunity" that need not exist, all because something inside the child needs to make a choice. The only choice you are offering is obedience or disobedience. You can be more creative than that!

Is this is a familiar experience for you? Try the following strategy several times, and see if you detect a different result. Instead of offering a choice to obey or not to obey, offer 2 choices that both involve being obedient. It could be as simple as, "When you go to bed in a minute, you can choose: Do you want to wear your red pajamas or your blue pajamas?" Or, "When you go to bed in a minute, you can choose whether to brush you teeth before or after you put on your pajamas." If it doesn't matter to you, let it matter to your child (and spouse too).

As a parent, you are focused on helping your children (whatever their style) become all they can be, but understand that you can't do it all for them. Many life lessons are learned through experience, and what your growing child needs from you is opportunity to grow "according to his own way," confident of your encouragement, loving correction, and understanding.

How does this apply to relations with your friends or spouse? Well, especially if *you* are the one with the most *D*, understand that they need opportunities to make choices and decisions too. Buy *them* some red pajamas!

Big kids at heart

I could write another 20 pages of stories demonstrating how using personal styles information has strengthened relationships at home and with friends.

I was privileged to attend the "re-wedding" of a couple whose divorce just didn't work out. He's a quiet guy who loves gardening. She's an upfront lady with a flashy convertible. (Her license tag holder reads, *"IT'S RED—IT'S FAST—IT'S MINE!"*) Misinterpreting their style differences tore them apart. This time around, understanding their differences is proving to be very helpful. It hasn't solved all of their challenges, but it provides them the daily option to begin again when they choose to do so.

I acknowledge that your head may be spinning from our zigzag course covering kids, spouses, unmet expectations, friends, and back to kids. Here's the thread: Whether you are a kid or an adult, your style's needs are predictable and significant. For instance, we discovered that a *D* child's need to be in charge can sometimes be satisfied by choosing between red or blue pajamas. This is not a big enough issue for a *D* adult, but the need for control and choice is still there.

What I'm suggesting is that many of the same needs must be addressed in all of our relationships. It's just the *scale* that's different—from simple to more complex. My real goal in this chapter has not been to tell interesting *stories* or provide one-size-fits-all *methods* that you can use on a moment's notice. Rather, I want you to use these events as tangible *examples* from real life, so you will believe that you can work out *your* relationship challenges too.

Look at every interaction with another individual from the perspective of **DISC**—yours and theirs. You can adjust to make the experience better for both of you. You can see the situation through their filters.

Finding success in personal relationships can involve spouses, children, family, or friends, but, again, most of the principles are the same. If your goal is building relationships that grow stronger over the years, make it your focus to become more skilled in adapting and adjusting to others.

If your goal is learning to respond more appropriately to people and situations, recognize your natural reactions, then identify more appropriate responses. Practice seeing people in terms of their *strengths,* rather than focusing on their areas of *struggle.* Give them dignity, respect, and acceptance. See them as companions, not as possessions.

Because we have covered a lot of territory in this section on personal relationships, here are the high points for review:

- Expectations are higher in dealing with family.
- Unmet expectations cause frustration and disagreement.
- Opposites attract and, eventually, they attack.

- We are born with certain style characteristics, and we develop others through environmental influences.
- We can teach our children according to their style.
- It is unfair to criticize or devalue people based on style issues because of our subjective understanding.
- We should deal with everyone, including our children, by understanding their style issues and our own.
- We can recognize an individual's life pattern, or "bent," even at an early age.
- We can *compete* by comparing our style differences, or we can *complete* by focusing on our style contributions.
- Men and women communicate differently (in addition to their style-based variations).
- Different styles make decisions and establish priorities differently.
- In matters of preference, we can agree to disagree, and we can provide what the other individual needs.

SECTION V: APPLICATIONS IN PROFESSIONAL RELATIONSHIPS

GETTING TO KNOW YOU

Chapter 18:
Finesse is Stronger
Than Force

From Chapter 16, you will recall these words of Cesare Pavese: "People don't remember *days;* they remember *moments.*" In teaching seminars, conducting workshops, and coaching teams, I have seen that few people remember the *details* of what I have said. Most often they remember how they *felt,* or reacted, when they heard it. They sometimes call out, "Say that again—it was good!"

"Memorable moments" was a guiding principle for Walt Disney too. Even in our interactions with friends and associates, we put more stock in our *perceptions* than in the actual words used in the exchange. This means there is real truth behind the cliché, "It's not what you say, but how you say it."

Dr. Paul Tournier, a Swiss psychiatrist and missionary, wrote, "He who loves, understands. He who understands, loves. One who feels understood feels loved, and one who feels loved feels sure of being understood." The progress of our personal and professional relationships is heavily influenced by the ways in which we respond to others, and they to us. The way people feel is a big deal!

With your new insights into your personal style, you are understanding that you can *choose* how you respond and how you interpret the responses of others. You have the ability to make people feel understood.

When time permits in my seminar, I like to create a "memorable moment." I ask a strong man from the audience to join me on the platform. I hand him several items: a length of 2x4 pine board, a square of sheetrock or drywall, a screw, and a hammer. My instructions are simple: attach the drywall to the board. In no time at all, the board is splintered, the drywall is damaged, and the screw is either bent or snapped in two.

Then I ask someone who is not so muscular to join me on the platform. I issue an identical set of materials, except that a screwdriver is substituted for the hammer. In moments, the drywall, the screw, and the board are securely joined, with no damage to any of the components. What could not be accomplished by force was achieved by finesse. And that's the moral of the story: often, finesse is more powerful than force!

Having the right tool for the job and possessing skill in using that tool are vital to your success. Psychologist Abraham Maslow said, "When the only tool you own is a hammer, every problem begins to resemble a nail." If your skills and tools are limited to hammering people into submission, you are one "leadership-challenged" individual! (Wasn't that a tactful phrase?) The harm inflicted in our drywall demonstration is comparable to the violence and damage we inflict on relationships and trust when we use force rather than finesse.

Before continuing, it's probably a good idea to define terms. I'm not using "finesse" in the sense of deception or manipulation. Rather, I mean dexterity, artfulness, skill, and a wise strategy. I mean a manner of dealing with people that enlists their cooperation and contributions.

Do you remember the story about the little boy who kept jumping out of his seat at school? His teacher had tried everything to keep him in place and, finally, she walked over to him, put her hands on his shoulders, and forced him down into his seat. The little boy looked up at her defiantly and mumbled, "I may be sitting down on the *outside*, but I'm still standing up on the *inside!*" You can use force to achieve compliance, but it's not cooperation.

Overcoming resistance

Maslow's Hierarchy of Needs shows that *fear of loss* is a stronger motivator than *hope of gain*. Most people are quicker to protect what they already have than they are to risk it for additional profit.

This is not always true among leaders, many of whom have **D** type styles. Sometimes it seems **D**s make changes just because they get bored with the status quo. But **D**s are outnumbered almost 5 to 1 by other types. Few followers (or employees) share their enthusiasm for change. To non-**D**s, change can be an uncertain threat.

But many **D** type leaders "encourage" others to cooperate with their plans for change by simply announcing that the rules have changed. *Force* says, "The old is dead, the future is now. This change is a revolution whose time has come." So the juggernaut has begun, and the slaves are expected to throw themselves under its wheels for the sake of progress!

Panic ensues among the "governed" as speculation mounts. Security and stability are threatened among those who have no power or leverage to limit these changes.

Force now steps forward to assure the frightened masses that he has taken their concerns into his thinking, and his plans are for everyone's best future. If this doesn't calm them, he tells the nervous that they can leave his company—he can get along without whiners and losers just fine! He may even dismiss some of the more expendable as examples to the rest. He decides that firings will continue until morale improves. Then he can't figure out why his employees don't trust him.

Speaker and author Mark Gorman puts it kindly when he says such people are "acluistic"—without a clue! All they have is a hammer, and they beat on everything until it either breaks or bends to their will.

How would *Finesse* handle the challenge of change? First, *Finesse* would recognize that change presents a threat of loss to most people. Change is not a positive motivator. *Finesse* wouldn't promote change; she would promote *"fix."* Who is afraid of *fix?* Very few! If something is broken or not working properly, *fix* is a good thing.

Finesse would also cause the leader to fix what needs fixing, but not change just for the sake of change. *Finesse* would ask tougher questions to find a *fix* than *Force* would ask to impose a change. She would also anticipate uneasiness and provide positive reassurances that demonstrate thoughtfulness and compassion. She would seek the counsel of those who had made a similar transition successfully. She would open channels of communication with all levels of personnel. *Finesse* would require the **D** leader to enlist **I** followers who would *inspire* others, **S** followers who would *support* others, and **C** followers who would move forward *carefully.*

The price of success

In my book, *The Price and the Prize,* I explain that 3 factors are always present in the price we pay to succeed in any endeavor:

- The price we pay is *always personal.* The leader's price and the follower's price are not the same; each pays a personal price that can't be compared to another's.

- The price we pay is *always costly.* It is weighed in terms of risk, change, and vulnerability, costing us the present to obtain a brighter future.

- The price we pay is *never negotiable.* Paying the full price *is* the shortcut. If the prize is worthy of its price, we should pay it. If it is not worthy of the full price, we should not bargain to obtain it.

How does this idea relate to the theme of finesse? In many situations, obtaining our desired prize requires the price of finesse. We must acquire valuable people skills rather than try to cheat or bully our way through using the power and leverage of force. If we recognize and respect that others will be required to pay their own price in following us, we must be willing to pay the full price of leading them.

In the long run, paying the full price to acquire these people tools and skills is a bargain. Finesse doesn't require nearly the energy that force demands. Its results call for much lower maintenance. When people merely submit to force, they must be closely watched and guarded. When people cooperate from the heart, they commit themselves to obtaining the desired result.

Why is it important to understand this Finesse Principle? Because, as we said at the beginning of the chapter, people remember moments. They remember feelings. They remember trust and understanding long beyond their memory of actual words. Indeed, finesse has power with people. And the power behind finesse is understanding the fears, wants, and needs of others' personal styles.

One size fits some

"People-smart" individuals don't use a cookie-cutter approach in dealing with others. They recognize the nuances in each person's style. They don't assume that all **D**s will always respond similarly. Style descriptors are not like bathrobes with a label reading ONE SIZE FITS ALL.

I deal more completely with strategies for understanding and meeting the needs of others in *The Price and the Prize*. The important concept for you to grasp now is that finesse is a powerful tool for building relationships.

Before we move on to "Success in Customer Service," I have included two pages explaining the basic premise behind Motivational Needs theories, the most famous of which is Maslow's. Interweaving personal style issues will help you fill in any gaps in your understanding of this topic.

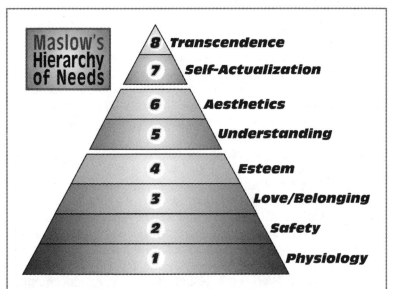

Abraham Maslow grouped human needs into 2 categories: DEFI-CIENCY (1–4 above) and GROWTH needs (5–8 above). He taught that **Physiological** needs (hunger, thirst, shelter, comfort) must be met before an individual's attention turns to the next higher level (**Safety/Security** needs). Likewise, the **Love/Belonging** needs (acceptance and affiliation with others) are not a priority until Physiological and Safety needs are met. **Esteem** needs (achievement, competence, approval, and recognition) are considered after the lower 3 are met.

According to Maslow, "higher" GROWTH needs can be acted on only if the "lower" DEFICIENCY needs are met first. If a deficiency recurs, the individual will act to correct it. Maslow said GROWTH needs follow a predetermined order: **Understanding** (knowledge and exploration), **Aesthetics** (symmetry, order, and beauty), **Self-Actualization** (finding fulfillment and realizing your potential) and, ultimately, **Transcendence** (helping others find self-fulfillment and realize their potential).

Other Motivational Needs theories abound. William James taught 3 levels: material, social, and spiritual. E. W. Mathes acknowledged a different 3: physiological, belongingness, and self-actualization. C. Alderfer identified the 3 levels as existence, relatedness, and growth.

Although these theories are taught as fact in many management courses, Maslow recognized that not all personality types align with his hierarchy. For instance, differences in motivational needs are easily observed between introverted and extroverted styles. The order in which we recognize our human needs can be influenced by our personal style. A task-oriented person may place a greater value on Understanding, while a people-oriented person may place greater value on Love and Belonging.

In an approach not focusing on needs, Frederick Herzberg, a psychologist and contemporary of Maslow's, proposed a theory about job factors that motivate employees. He said company policies, supervision, interpersonal relations, working conditions, and salary are "Hygiene Factors" rather than motivators. Accordingly, absence of Hygiene Factors can create job dissatisfaction, but their presence does not motivate or create satisfaction. Instead, he reported 5 factors as strong determiners of job satisfaction: **Achievement**, **Recognition**, the **Work** itself, **Responsibility**, and **Advancement**.

Herzberg said "Satisfiers," or motivators, are associated with long-term positive effects in job performance, while Hygiene Factors ("Dissatisfiers") consistently produce only short-term changes in job attitudes and performance. Satisfiers relate to what the person does, while Dissatisfiers relate to the situation in which the persons does it.

My point in referring to these various hierarchy models is this: any cookie-cutter version of a Needs Hierarchy is incomplete as a consistent, all-encompassing answer to the question, "How do I motivate people to do what needs to be done?"

In practical terms, expect priority within any Needs Hierarchy to differ from individual to individual. A generic approach that presumes to know what people want next fails to consider varieties of personal style. In fact, according to the Educational Resources Information Center, individuals often have problems consistently articulating what they want from a job. Compounding the question, many managers consistently ignore what individuals say they want, but instead tell employees what they want based on a hierarchy chart.

Learning how to ask the right questions, being sensitive to style issues, and understanding issues of need are finesse tools that will more easily bring your "board, sheetrock, and screw" together.

Chapter 19: Success in Customer Service

In the next few chapters, we'll be focusing on specific areas of business productivity. Some readers will be tempted to rationalize that they have no need for such knowledge because they are involved in a high-tech or product-based business, instead of a high-touch or people-based business. My first task will be to help those readers understand that their ongoing success will be heavily influenced by whether or not they understand and embrace this information.

In the Preface, I mentioned an oft-quoted study reporting that 15% of success in finding a job in your desired career, keeping that job, and moving ahead in your career relates directly to *technical* knowledge and skills, while 85% of success relates to knowledge and skills with *people*.

Since these statistics were cited by Zig Ziglar in his 1986 book, *Top Performance* (Old Tappan, NJ; Fleming H. Revell Company), some managers question its validity in today's high-tech work environments. There's a tendency among some in the 21st Century to think that flipping a calendar page and announcing a new millennium means that all of the old rules go away. Actually, this is *not* thinking at all.

As an example, the e-commerce explosion at the end of

the last century had many people believing that "tech" had successfully repealed everything we used to know about business and economics. In our New Economy, some investors thought it was impossible for stock prices to drop. From that point on, stocks could only rise, and they would do so dramatically. Everything "dotcom" was assured of succeeding, as traditional brick-and-mortar continued to fade into memory. The coming Age of the Geek would make 1999 as quaint and irrelevant as Victorian times.

Talk about unmet expectations! Many who thought they were creating the tides have discovered that they were only riding a wave. I'm not pessimistic about the future, but past lessons, learned and proved in the midst of great difficulty, remain valid until further notice. Bluntly put, disregarding the importance of *one-on-one relationships* in current and future commerce is inviting trouble.

In transacting business, products and services are incapable of moving themselves out the door. People—buyers and sellers—move them. *People* need products; *products* don't need products. *People* buy products; *products* don't buy products. The demands that *people* place on a product give it value.

If the inexperienced and the unwise in business are devaluing people skills and emphasizing only technical skills, it's because this is what they believe consumers are buying the most of right now, or because it's easier to *produce a competitive product* than to *render a competitive service*.

Competition is fierce, with businesses trying to wrestle their share of customer dollars from the fickle folks who do the buying. Competitors are pushing to find whatever product is in demand and move it now, using faster and cheaper ways to get it through *their* doors and out to consumers. I believe that *winning customers* is better, long-term, than *finding consumers.*

What your customers want

Through business mentors, I learned that companies don't succeed if they only sell *products* and don't provide *service.* A hardware retailer announced that, while his company had sold over a million quarter-inch drill bits the year before, they had not sold even *one* to a customer who actually wanted the product. What every customer wanted was the *by-product:* customers wanted quarter-inch *holes.* The retailer was not *selling bits* but *providing holes. Service* is the bottom line for a company seeking profitability.

Can you think of a successful business that doesn't provide a valuable service to its customers? In their book, *The 22 Immutable Laws of Marketing: Violate Them at Your Own Risk* (New York, NY; HarperBusiness, 1994), Al Ries and Jack Trout explain that, in the New Economy, businesses of every kind have become your competition because customers are growing more and more experienced and discriminating about the service they receive.

Similarly, in Tom Connellan's book, *Inside the Magic Kingdom: 7 Keys to Disney's Success* (Austin, TX; Bard Press, 1997) the author claims that if any company's service department answers telephone calls on the fourth ring, and then places callers on hold for 5 minutes, Federal Express has become its competitor for customer satisfaction. FedEx's customer calls are answered on the first ring and quickly directed to live assistance on request. Any other company's customers who have experienced this level of service with FedEx know that this is possible to achieve. Other businesses could meet this standard too, if customer service became a high enough priority. So your company's biggest competitor for customer satisfaction may be an entirely different standard in an entirely different industry.

Here's a key question: if you recognized an opportunity to improve your customers' perceptions about the value of your product or service, wouldn't you be smart to take advantage of it?

Identify your "other" customers

Businesses seem to rise and fall on customer satisfaction. A number of years ago, my company was a contract show producer for "live" theme park audiences across the country. In one park, I thought that we were very successful, because Guest Relations comments about our shows were positive and, in the park's guest surveys, we were praised 6 times more frequently than all other shows combined. I wrongly believed that pleasing the guests would assure us a spot in the lineup for years.

My mistake was in thinking that the *guests* were *my* customers. Really, they were the *park's* customers, and the park's Operations Department was my *only* customer. I did not tend, or guard, that relationship well, while my competitors cultivated it. Eventually, they won my contract. Was their production as good? Judging from guest evaluations, I don't think it was, but my competition made the *real customer* happier.

Your suppliers as customers

With the introduction of just-in-time manufacturing and delivery, a company's suppliers must now be courted as if they are customers. Your company may be bringing your suppliers business, but suppliers provide what your company needs, and it might not take much to bump your needs farther down their priority list, if competition heats up. Although the TV show M*A*S*H has been out of production for years, you probably know the character of Corporal Radar O'Reilly. He was an Iowa farmboy who always knew what the commanding officer wanted, even before being asked. He was able to get Sparky, the supply officer, on the phone in moments, find whatever the M*A*S*H. unit needed, and arrange a bargain price. He had supply connections everywhere, and he established them by using his people skills.

Have you been thinking of vendors and suppliers as your servants or as your customers? How are your people skills in this area? How does your company's attitudes toward your suppliers assist or hinder them in providing what you need?

Your employees as customers

In the New Economy, skilled employees who provide consistent results are a valuable commodity sought after by other businesses. The cost of retaining your workforce and their loyalty is small when compared to the cost of finding and training replacements. Considering the time, effort, and money that most companies spend attracting and keeping customers, it's amazing how little money some companies spend in keeping and attracting employees. Zig

Ziglar has addressed a concern of many business owners: *what if I spend money improving employees' performance, and then they leave me, hired away by another company?* Zig answers that it is worse, in the long run, *not* to train them and have them *stay!*

In the old days, many employees worked for one company throughout their entire career. I have a cousin who worked for one employer for $18^1/_2$ years. Eventually, the company eliminated his entire division, and he trained for a new career. After a few months, he found that the work didn't fit his personal style, so he began circulating his résumé. I was amazed that he worried whether a potential employer might think he was unstable in his work history, since he had so recently dropped an unsatisfying job. In today's job market, some companies think applicants are unstable if they have stayed too long in one place!

Recent changes in the ways employers and employees relate are causing many workers to view themselves as self-employed. They feel much more in charge of their futures than workers of the past. Those who seek advancement are pursuing outside education, upgrading their training and certifications, and hiring private coaches to help them manage their careers.

How should these changes cause companies to treat this precious resource, their employees? How should they woo these "customers" who are increasingly seeing the labor and skills they provide as a business-to-business service?

Your employer as a customer

Likewise, some wise employees are treating their managers as customers to be won, serviced, and kept. They recognize that the manager's patronage and goodwill is worth cultivating. In times of corporate downsizing, rightsizing, and capsizing, well-placed loyalties can make a difference in being retained, retrained, or referred successfully. Career-minded workers know that being properly aligned in an organization can make the difference between survival and the unemployment line, and many are actively recruiting the loyalty of their managers and servicing their needs.

Your coworkers as customers

Let's draw this out one more level, to include other employees and departments within a company. I have consulted with corporations whose biggest supply bottleneck occurs between their sales and production divisions. A salesperson may promise something that the company can't produce within the required time frame, thereby angering "internal partners," who resent being made to appear incompetent. Or a production manager may anger the company's traffic manager, who schedules deliveries all across their distribution network. In retaliation, a pallet of parts sits on the shipping dock for an extra 3 days. Production falls behind schedule, the salesperson must call the end-customer to make excuses for the delay, and the customer cancels the order because another company can provide what is needed now.

What should it be worth to a company to keep communication open between coworkers, employers, employees, suppliers, and customers? Because service really is any company's ultimate product, its worth is...priceless!

Getting the results you want

Business consultant, speaker, and author Alan Weiss tells about a man who lost his luggage on a business trip. The traveler stormed into the baggage claim office, demanding that something be done immediately. Under stress, he was rude and impatient with the employee taking his information. Eventually, the baggage clerk responded, "Sir, at this moment, there are only 2 people in the world who know, or care, about your missing bag—and one of them is rapidly losing interest!"

There are times in business, and in lost luggage, when only *someone else* has the ability to get you what you want or need. Can you see that, when you need help from others, your *high-touch* skills count at least as much as your high-tech abilities? There will always be a demand for those who have *finesse* with people.

For decades, Zig Ziglar has preached to business leaders that the greatest and surest way to get what you want in life, or in business, is by being able to help others get what they want. And the way I see it, if Zig said it, it must be true!

Chapter 20:
Success in Sales

In this chapter, we'll consider some of the elements of a sales presentation that can be positively affected by understanding and adjusting your personal style. I don't make my living in sales, so I won't presume to instruct you on the *techniques* of selling. Numerous books are available that document successful, proven methods of making a sale. I only want to help you think about *why* your customer would want to buy from *you*, whatever you are selling.

In terms of Maslow's Hierarchy (*Pages 193–194*), is what you have to offer an answer to a DEFICIENCY need or a GROWTH need? Whether it's a *survival* item or an *enhancement* item, there are *style-specific needs* and *fears* to which you can appeal (*Pages 99–101*), as shown below. The more closely you can target your presentation to address these issues, the more effect and influence you will have with your customer.

BASIC STYLE'S FEAR			
D	**I**	**S**	**C**
being used unfairly by others	loss of social acceptance	confrontation and change in routine	unpredictable outcomes, risk
BASIC STYLE'S NEEDS & MOTIVATORS			
CONTROL	**RECOGNITION**	**APPRECIATION**	**INFORMATION**
choice, challenge, authority, variety, freedom, prestige	acceptance, interaction, approval, fun, status	assurance, closure, inclusion, specialization, harmony	accuracy, logic, procedures, value, security

Influence is the name of the game in sales, and it springs from how much credibility you have with the customer. The more you can show customers that you understand their unspoken concerns, and that you have similar values and attitudes, the more they will feel kinship and confidence.

Years ago, our office received a letter praising a program representative (*salesman*) who had introduced our motivational presentations for family audiences to a school principal. He said that Roger was very different from other salespeople who called on him. Roger, he said, *became a friend* who asked about the problems the principal dealt with as an educator, offered helpful feedback, and then introduced our program as a focused solution for several issues. He bought our service because Roger was a credible, good guy. Yes, we spent a good deal of money on promotional materials to back Roger's efforts, but other representatives used the same materials with less success. People bought from him because they liked him and felt he understood and liked them too. Roger *himself* was the difference!

In short, people in sales add tangible value to their company and its product or service. Chances are that prospects will never tour the factory or sit down with the president. They will make their decisions based on how they feel about you!

Numerous factors can work in your favor, including being aware of your style's tendencies, structuring your actions and words to more closely correspond to the style of your customer, and creating a comfortable environment in which the customer is more willing to agree with you. Here are 3 pages of charts, showing how you can adapt yourself for greater success in dealing with the 4 basic types.

BUYER'S PROFILE			
ATTRACTED TO INNOVATIVE PRODUCTS	**ATTRACTED TO SHOWY PRODUCTS**	**ATTRACTED TO TRADITIONAL PRODUCTS**	**ATTRACTED TO PROVEN PRODUCTS**
Quick decider, strong ego.	Impulsive decider, wants approval.	Slow decider, wants friendship.	Cautious decider, wants details.
A multitasking entrepreneur.	A socializer and storyteller.	Family oriented and shy.	Value-oriented and suspicious.
Appreciates innovative design.	Wants to try things out.	Wants the "known" over the "new."	Looks for inaccurate statements.
SELLER'S BEST APPROACH TO BUYER			
Present the high points and the bottom line.	Present energetically to make the best impression.	Pace your approach and take it easy.	Present proof, results, and background.
Provide services that take care of the details.	Provide personalized follow-up and service.	Provide statistics and demonstrate reliability.	Provide rational, unemotional testimonials.
Solution-driven.	Emotion-driven.	Relationship-driven.	Quality-driven.
Not motivated by testimonials, data, or details.	Not motivated by details, but by endorsement.	Not motivated by deadlines or insistence.	Not motivated by concepts or ideas, but by facts.
HOW SELLER CAN CREATE A CONDUCIVE ENVIRONMENT			
Get down to business.	Recognize and praise their efforts.	Chat about family and personal life.	Avoid chatter and emotionalism.
Provide direct answers.	Provide time for socializing.	Provide sincere responses.	Provide a detailed package.
Acknowledge their accomplishments.	Bring them back to the topic using their own words.	Answer their questions with simple examples.	Be understated in your comments and opinions.
Ask for their feedback and opinion.	Ask how they feel about ideas.	Ask what their concerns are.	Ask them to decide for themselves.
Emphasize challenge, rewards, and results.	Summarize and connect important points.	Empathize with their desire to serve others well.	Itemize the benefits of deciding soon.

TYPICAL QUESTIONS IN THE BUYER'S MIND

"What does it cost?"	"Is there flexibility in the price?"	"Why should I switch now?"	"Is this a proven product?"
"When can I get it?"	"Is there a payment plan?"	"What if it doesn't work for me?"	"What is your warranty?"
"Is this the latest version?"	"Who else is doing this?"	"What is its track record or history?"	"How does this compare to others?"
"Is this your best model?"	"Can we discuss this over coffee?"	"Is this all I need, or are there add-ons?"	"This isn't a new idea, is it?"
"Can I change or upgrade it?"	"What's in it for me to do this?"	"How good is your warranty?"	"How are your people qualified?"
"Do you really believe what you are telling me?"	"How will doing it make me look good?"	"My supplier gives good service—why should I change?"	"How long has your company been in business?"
"How will this free me for more important pursuits?"	"Will I enjoy doing this, or will it be more work and responsibility?"	"How difficult will it be to switch over, and is there assistance?"	"Will this product be able to match my exact specifications?"

SELLER'S CLOSING TECHNIQUES

Provide a choice between 2 options, both of which are favorable, but offer this customer a sense of control.	Close quickly, providing a choice between 2 or 3 options, each of which will result in this customer feeling good about saying "Yes" to the sale.	Offer a chance to try it personally before making a decision, and involve their family or team in its usefulness and benefits.	Recommend an opportunity to test its suitability in the environment where it will be used. Acknowledge and affirm your customer's criteria.
Take choice away by suggesting that it may be out of their budget, or that they may not be "quite ready" for all its benefits at this time.	Paint a picture of acknowledgment and recognition, based on their success in making this good decision.	Ask for a small, no-risk deposit that will help you hold the product, or deal, so they can give themselves time to think about it.	Suggest a small, no-risk deposit that will freeze the terms while they take time to check the supplied information.

SELLER'S APPROACHES TO MOTIVATING THE BUYER

"You are just the type of person who can really make this work."	"You have the ability to work with this futuristic idea."	"You can call some others who have made the switch."	"You will value the quality with which we have designed this."
"You'll be in control of what happens."	"You'll be seen as a trendsetter with this."	"You'll increase your security by doing this."	"You can determine this for yourself."
"This identifies you as a leader in your industry."	"You obviously have an eye on the future."	"We back our work with a 100% guarantee."	"We can meet with your team to look at the facts."
"You can call this your own and get the credit for what your work has accomplished."	"We may even be able to use you and the company as a showcase for how well this works."	"We have been doing this for years, so you can depend on our being here when you need us."	"When I leave here today, I want to have answered all of your questions in complete detail."

APPROACHES THAT DEMOTIVATE THE BUYER

Appearing tentative, unsure, or indecisive.	Appearing cold or too businesslike in your approach.	Appearing to be in a hurry or rushing them.	Appearing to be shallow or vague about details.
Dodging an objection or challenge.	Trivializing their comments or concerns.	Being overly friendly from the beginning.	Touching them when you first meet.
Explaining details or involved statistics.	Explaining in a complicated manner.	Skipping details or not having ready answers.	Generalizing, rather than being specific.
Stating your opinion as a source of influence.	Not allowing them to share their enthusiasm.	Criticizing your competitors.	Exaggerating success or benefits.
Setting limits.	Creating a setting in which they can talk themselves out of the sale or run out of time.	Closing too soon.	Over-enthusiasm.
Failing to cater to ego or provide personal attention.		Becoming too loud or emotional, being too physical, or invading their space.	Being too familiar, or breaching a confidence in demonstrating friendship.

How they say your name

For several years, I advised McDonald's Corporation on its use of Ronald McDonald® as an entertainer and goodwill ambassador around the world. I was fascinated by the great number of Americans who know that McDonald's sells fast food, but they don't think of it as a restaurant. Instead, *"McDonald's"* is the best way to describe it—in a class by itself. Part of the reason for this is the way the corporation has positioned itself and its stores in the consumer's mind. Almost from the beginning, it was a "McHappy Place" and "Your Kind of Place." It was one of the first businesses to put in playgrounds for small customers. Ronald uses sign language in his commercials to acknowledge deaf kids. Ronald McDonald House is a widely supported charity that provides a home-away-from-home for the families of hospitalized children.

McDonald's has enjoyed *name recognition* for a long time, but they continue doing all of these things, and more, to build *name appreciation.* How does your sales force build *appreciation,* rather than just *knowledge,* about your company? The way your customers "taste" it, as your company's name rolls across their tongues, is a big part of selling. As customers say your name, how does it taste to them?

Don't lose sight of the last paragraph's significance, but let's take this idea one step further. McDonald's does more than show pride in its reputation; it defends that reputation. The people who produce Koala Kare diaper changing stations for restrooms knew they couldn't make their case if the customer was on the defensive, so, when it was time for their appointment to demonstrate their product to

McDonald's decision-making team, they simply set up their display, showed how it worked and how little space it required, and then they shared endorsements from some franchise stores that were already using the equipment successfully.

The result? No one on the committee shouted, "*Eureka! This is what we've been looking for!*" (After all, how many McDonald's executives change baby diapers in a restroom stall?) Drawing the presentation to a close, the presenter asked if there were any questions from the committee. One person raised a hand and asked, "I think you left something out—what's the doll for, over there in the corner on the floor?" The presenter paused and then said, "That's where mothers have to change their babies at McDonald's now."

This appeal to McDonald's pride was not hostile, as a frontal attack would have been. It was as sensitively—and powerfully—handled as possible. The corporation's response was to buy 2 for each of their stores—one for the ladies' restroom and one for the men's.

This story would have fit nicely in Chapter 18, but it's here to help me illustrate several successful sales principles:

- The sales team recognized the client's pride in reputation and their need to protect it
- They subtly appealed to the client's fear of loss
- They didn't insult the client, but provided opportunity for them to discover their need on their own
- They created a memorable moment that solidified the message in the client's mind

Did the Koala Kare company officer who told me this story

understand personal styles? I don't think so. So you *can* succeed without this knowledge but, if I had to compete against a team as sharp as they were, *I* would want to know everything I could about **DISC**. I would want every advantage!

DISC on purpose

There are many successful companies that include personal styles workshops as part of their sales training. It is a service offered by my company and others. The following examples demonstrate how effective this training can be when used appropriately.

- An auto dealership's general manager is quoted in the book *DISC: The Universal Language* relating the success his sales force achieved after being trained for only six hours in "Behavioral Selling Skills." In the weekend after training, the dealership shattered its all-time daily record. It followed up by breaking its monthly record, and then its all-time weekly record! The manager reported, "We no longer sell cars. We work to make people happy!"

Is **DISC** knowledge some kind of magic wand? No, but not even a wand makes anything happen until the magician picks it up and waves it around. Unless you put it to use, you won't see anything amazing from your book-level familiarity with personal styles.

- A participant in a multilevel business moved, in 3 months, from 65 associates and $7,000 in monthly group sales to 78 associates and more than $18,000 in monthly volume. She reported an increase of more than 150% by using people skills to encourage the strengths of those in her organization. Addressing the needs, wants, and goals of her team provided energy and fueled their desire to move ahead. Getting what *they* wanted also got her what *she* wanted.

One of the great benefits of understanding personal styles is how being able to use this information to unlock people's undiscovered gifts and abilities. You not only learn how to understand and motivate yourself, but you become able to help others understand and motivate themselves.

- Another car dealership success story involves a salesperson with an **S** type style. (Most people don't think of **S**s as a being good in sales. After all, they aren't fast talkers who push to close a deal, but they certainly can succeed.) He was showing a new Pontiac to a couple and, because of his training in **DISC**, he recognized that both partners showed intense **C** traits. When they announced that they were really interested in a comparable Ford, he knew they were doing research to support their comfort with a decision they had already made. He also knew that people tend to buy from those whose styles are similar to their own. So, confident of his product and knowing that he would lose them if they felt any "pitch" or pressure, he offered them quality information and printed resources.

Then, knowing that they were headed to a nearby Ford dealership, he referred them to a salesman who had a much more aggressive **D** style and who knew nothing about adapting his style to fit better with customers. True to form, the Ford salesman was assertive in trying to make the couple buy on the spot. After doing more research, the couple bought the Pontiac from the salesperson who seemed more like themselves. In this instance, the *buyer* decided that the *seller* was more important than a *brand name*.

Was the Pontiac salesperson manipulating people and circumstances? Was he simply using the existing rules of the game to win? Did his approach to the customers harm them or keep information from them?

Focus on your own needs

Where do you need help in selling successfully? Do you and the salespeople in your organization understand style-oriented sales and service? If you understood before picking up this book, perhaps they did too. Until now, how would you have answered this question:

WHO, AMONG YOUR SALES PROSPECTS AND CLIENTS NEEDS:
- **Bullet points and opportunity to negotiate?**
- **Fun and personal contact?**
- **Proven products and assurance?**
- **Specific data and time to think?**

Now, because of what you have learned about **DISC**, you not only know *who* needs *what*, but you know *how* you can adapt and adjust to give it to them!

Chapter 21:
Success in
Negotiating

I am not a born negotiator. I'm *naturally* more of a born appeaser. My *I* really wants to be accepted and validated, and my **S** wants to avoid conflict and bring harmony to my environment. I always thought *negotiating* was *making* the other guy do what I want. (Usually, this is seen as a **D** type skill because **D**s can make a round peg fit in a square hole if they have enough time and a big enough hammer.)

I've read several books on negotiation skills that focus on acting like an unadjusted **D**. They seem to be based on the idea that *my* winning means *someone else* has to lose. I want win–win solutions, in which all of us get much of what we want and believe that we have exchanged value for value. I resent feeling manipulated or pushed, and I will only work in such an atmosphere if I am compelled.

Among some people, I've just disqualified myself from commenting about negotiation skills. Win–lose myths prevail in their mindset and decree, "Never give a sucker an even break!" However, if you could choose between *extorting compliance from* people, or *negotiating cooperation with* people, which would you rather have?

Every day, people with different styles and approaches

demonstrate that they can be good negotiators. Using the *strengths* of their styles:

- *D* types can build a *dream* and *vision* that supersedes old rivalries.
- *I* types can *involve, influence,* and *inspire* people.
- *S* types, who dislike conflict, can bring differing sides together by addressing common interests.
- *C* types can analyze details that keep people apart and identify the key areas to address objectively.

Truly, the effectiveness of a negotiator is in his or her ability to affect others.

Get comfortable, and get a "yes"

Do you remember the joke about the patient who swung his arm over his head and said, "Doc, it hurts when I do this." His doctor replied, "Then don't do that!"

This is also the best prescription an amateur like me can offer you about negotiating. Identify the style of those you are negotiating with, recognize their hot buttons, and *don't push them—unless you mean to!*

We have identified where each type most easily feels threatened and how they tend to respond when threatened. (*Hint: never use the word "cooperative" to describe their response!*) If you want to hear them say Yes, create a comfortable environment rather than an hostile atmosphere.

Many times, negotiations succeed through teamwork when they would not have succeeded alone. If at all possible, don't strategize independently. Instead, team up with other styles different from your own, and cover as many bases as possible. Accept feedback from your team members, who, because of their diversity, will have filters and viewpoints that differ. Return again and again to what you know about personal styles.

During the Viet Nam war, negotiations were impeded when no one could agree on the shape of the table. Finally the announcement came that the final decision was "round." If possible, I would prefer to sit at a table with only *one* side. All of us would sit together on that side. Then, the only thing opposite us would be the problem we were trying to fix.

I don't really expect those I'm negotiating with to come sit on my side, but I want to move past the "sides" issue and get to the nitty-gritty of what is separating us. At the least, I put myself *mentally* on their side of the table and, when the situation allows, I try to avoid sitting *opposite* them, with an artificial barrier between us.

The seating diagram at the top of the next page shows the *natural* comfort zone for the person you're negotiating with or selling to. You can see that, for *task-oriented* customers, buyers, clients, and others, their most comfortable positioning is *across* from you. **D**s want "control" distance, and **C**s want "objectivity" distance. Most *people-oriented* individuals prefer closer contact, allowing them to "feel" your attitude.

My preference is to try for just a little closer contact, rather than sitting across from the client. I don't really expect the adjacent "*I* position" to happen often, but I want the 90° "**S** position· whenever I can get it.

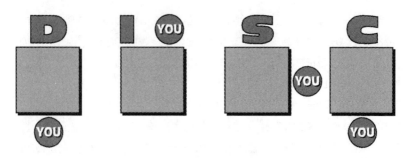

From my years as a show producer, I know that having audience members sitting close to each other creates more receptivity and responsiveness. Think of it as "gapping" a spark plug. You want just enough distance to get the best spark, but too much, or too little, will cause a misfire and loss of energy. The key to *close proximity comfort* for **D**s and **C**s is to respect the space you have permitted them to have, and to be very careful in exercising emotional and physical restraint, so that you don't overwhelm their control or objectivity needs.

In addition to physical distance, consider *verbal* distance. When presenting your message to a group that is large enough to require a platform or a microphone, avoid *"You Out There"* language. This occurs *verbally* when you separate yourself *mentally* from your audience. Those who are not on stage become "You Out There" (as in, "How many of *You Out There* are ready to sign this contract and get back to work?") Since everyone is under the same roof, use inclusive terms. Find ways to express *"Us In Here."* Use "we" and "you," as if you are talking to one person. Outsiders never feel comfortable. Physically, verbally, and mentally, we need to bring people together to reach consensus.

We can isolate with the written word too. Recently, I re-

ceived an e-mail response in which the writer unintention-
ally suggested distance between us. His note began with
this phrase: *"Chris, you and I are 180° apart on this..."* I responded to his note with an e-mail that began, *"I don't know,
Rick, that YOU and I are ever 180° on anything. Our VIEWS
may differ, but I never see US as opposed. I hope you agree."*
It's important that our physical and verbal approaches build
bridges, not walls.

We tend to think of negotiating as the final effort for
settlement before a union lockout. What I'm suggesting is
that negotiating happens all the time, but we don't always
call it by that name. Resolving any disagreement favorably
requires openness, trust, and cooperation.

Since we're talking about negotiating skills, let's take a
moment to talk about *accountability*. It means being willing
to explain your actions and motivations to others, as well as
bear the rewards or consequences of the outcome. When
we build people of integrity into our lives—people who hold
us accountable—we gain the ability to maintain balance and
perspective. These are people who remember what we have
said and promised, and they stay around to remind us and
help us keep our word. There is tremendous protection in
being held accountable.

Let me tie accountability and negotiation together for you.
My friend, Alan Ross, is president of Corporate Development
Institute. He told me about a company whose strong-willed
president had exercised unchecked use of his power and alien-
ated his employees. To save the company from financial ruin,
Alan was brought in to negotiate concessions from the Union
regarding the workers' contract. As signs of good faith, the

corporate officers turned in their luxury cars. They scaled back on expenses and salaries. They surrendered the executive parking lot, so his top people contended with the muddy employee lot on rainy days just as Union members did.

Trust was being reestablished—a vital element if employees were going to believe the company had turned over a new leaf. Only one person was unwilling to go along with the plan—the president. He must have *needed* his luxury car and parking space more than he needed loyal employees. Because his actions announced his attitude, employees resented him tremendously and distrusted any proposed changes.

At the negotiating table with Union officials, Alan explained his plan and the Union concessions that would allow it to work. No one would lose a job, but some workers would be moved around within the company as certain tasks were automated. There was a true feeling of trust and cooperation in the boardroom until, at a key moment, everyone saw the president drive up to the building in his luxury car and park in his private space. Literally, all good will ended at that moment, and anger refocused on that leader, who was incapable of leading.

Read whatever books will help you hone your skills to become a sharp negotiator. At the same time, remember what people want, what they need, and how their filters work as they see, hear, and feel your message. Be aware of why you need accountability for your actions, and what, in your personal style, feels threatened at that prospect. Commit to becoming a win–win negotiator.

Chapter 22: Success in Hiring and Managing

Used wisely, there is a definite role for **DISC** to play on the job. The federal government's Equal Employment Opportunity Commission (EEOC) exists to keep the playing field level for job applicants and workers. Discrimination comes in odd packages, so, while it's helpful to understand a potential employee's personal style, and how he or she may fit best in your organization, it's not permissible to use a style assessment instrument as *the* deciding criterion for employment decisions. No producer of assessments has ever demonstrated that a psychological test or personnel screening questionnaire is an accurate predictor of an applicant's ability to succeed at a given task. There are tests of knowledge that can be correlated to work duties, but it's unlawful for an employer to say, "I think a **C** is what I need, so send every applicant home who doesn't fit the profile."

Nevertheless, this government rule does not preclude your gathering as much performance-based information as possible on applicants and employees so you can help them do a better job or form better teams. Here are several ways you can legally use information from a Personal Style Assessment Report in your workplace:

BENCHMARKING: Work Environment

Steps to Create a Benchmark for the Work Environment:

Identify Managers and Workers to Profile About Position

Process and Profile Assessment Instruments

Identify and Discuss Similarities for Benchmarking

Adjust and Create Final Benchmark Report

File Report for Future Use

BENCHMARKING: Job Behavior

Benchmark the Job Behavior in 2 Steps:

(1) Identify 8 to 10 Top / Bottom Workers in this Position

Compare Reports of the Top 3 Workers

Compare Reports to Environment Master Report

Identify Similarities in Top 3 Workers Reports

Document Behaviors. Use Similarities in Selection Process

(2) Have Workers Complete Style Analysis Form

Compare Reports of the Bottom 3 Workers

Compare Reports to Environment Master Report

Identify Similarities in Bottom 3 Workers Reports

Document Behaviors. Do Not Use Them in Selection Process

BENCHMARKING: Job Selection

Benchmark the Work Environment

Interview Applicants

Benchmark Successful Workers Styles

Assess Applicant's Personal Style and Environment

Compare Results to Benchmark

Collect Top Candidates for Final Decision

Interview and Rank Top Candidates

Notify Candidates of Selection

BENCHMARKING: Team Development

All Team Members Complete Assessment Forms

Style Reports Processed by Computer

DISC Explained and Reports are Reviewed

Teams Learn DISC Communication Do's and Dont's

Small Groups Practice Problem-Solving and Report Success

Show How Styles Influenced Problem Solving

- *Benchmarking* measures common factors found in your most successful or productive workers. A report, or profile, identifies skills or traits that many of the top producers share. Use this information to improve quality-control efforts, to train others in how to be more effective, and to assign workers to tasks and teams that make good use of their particular strengths.

Benchmarking can also be used to establish an ideal work environment, or to establish criteria for job applicants, if you can demonstrate the direct application of the results to job performance. (For example, if you are a school principal wanting to hire a new chemistry teacher, part of your benchmark criteria might be a degree in education, which can be shown to have a direct bearing on the applicants' ability to do the job.)

Personal style assessments, team composition studies, and occupational benchmarking work well together. The progressive charts *(left)* show some steps in the process.

- *Job Performance Reviews* are often performed annually, and a manager evaluates an employee's productivity and success in performing the job's functions. Typically, these appraisals are *subjective*, often based on assumptions and style conflicts. Because they occur only once or twice a year, a lot of pent-up tension can emerge, and many companies view this process as more destructive than instructive.

However, *objectivity* is introduced into Job Performance Reviews when the manager and the worker can sit together and examine the strengths and struggles of the employee's personal style and work habits. A less defensive atmosphere is created because the report is the subject of the meeting, and the participants are able to agree on a plan of improvement that includes action steps, measurable results, time-sensitive feedback, and follow-through with accountability.

• *Team contributions* can be matched to assemble more effective work groups, allowing greater productivity and harmony. When managers are able to refer to each employee's Personal Style Assessment Report, they can identify the individuals whose contributions will enhance a specific project. As group members are enabled to understand, use, and appreciate each other's special abilities, contributions, and perspectives, a true team identity begins to emerge.

T•E•A•M Contributions

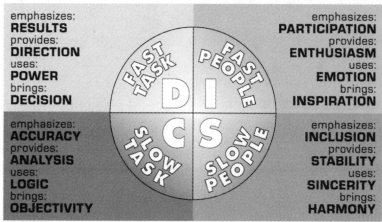

emphasizes:
RESULTS
provides:
DIRECTION
uses:
POWER
brings:
DECISION

emphasizes:
PARTICIPATION
provides:
ENTHUSIASM
uses:
EMOTION
brings:
INSPIRATION

emphasizes:
ACCURACY
provides:
ANALYSIS
uses:
LOGIC
brings:
OBJECTIVITY

emphasizes:
INCLUSION
provides:
STABILITY
uses:
SINCERITY
brings:
HARMONY

Together Everyone Achieves More

Chapter 23: Success in Leadership

We're switching gears here to look at effective leadership, with **DISC** styles in mind. As with negotiation skills, many people think the skills for effective leadership occur naturally in **D** type people, making them the best leaders. There are numerous books on leadership that could have as their subtitle, *"How to Be a **D** and Be Like Me!"* I am thankful that I was directed to several authors who don't embrace this approach. If you're interested in reading more about the development of effective leaders, a few of my favorite books are mentioned in the final chapter.

Leadership is all about style, but it doesn't depend on your having one particular personal style. It depends on learning to use your own style in effective and appropriate ways, so that you become attractive to people, who, in turn, accept your leadership and align with your goals and action plan. Your ability to attract and influence people is a big part of being a leader. As John Maxwell says, "If you think you're leading, but nobody's following, you're just out for a walk!" What makes a leader attractive to others?

- Some people are attracted by the *strength* and *determination* of their leader. (These are intense **D** traits.)

- Many people are attracted by *persuasiveness* and *optimism,* which are *I* type leadership qualities.
- Others are attracted by the *servant-heart* and *steadiness* that typify *S* leaders.
- Still others are attracted by the *trustworthiness* and *sober demeanor* of leaders who have intense *C* traits.

A leader requires more than charisma. "Staying power" is more important, because a leader who gets his followers all fired up and then runs out of fuel is no leader at all. I enjoy hearing about political and military leaders of the past, and how their personal styles influenced their victories and defeats. Knowing what you now know about style issues, you might enjoy watching George C. Scott's amazing portrayal as the star of *Patton.* The film captures the personal styles of most leaders in World War II, and now you'll understand why they acted as they did.

If you are a *Bible* reader, you'll find many clues about the personal styles of Abraham, Moses, David, David's son, Solomon, and others, as you read the accounts of their lives in the Old Testament. In the New Testament, you can do the same with Jesus' disciples and the Apostles. You will observe most about their styles by identifying their responses to stressful situations. For instance, Saint Paul asserts himself with a very in-charge *D* style, while Saint Peter has very impulsive *I* type reactions. Saint John has so many *S* qualities that he's the only disciple who shows up to comfort Jesus' mother, Mary, at the Crucifixion. Saint Thomas doubts the Resurrection, and displays *C* type behavior whenever he is mentioned during his time following Jesus. My friend, Ken

Voges, has written extensively on the **DISC** factors that influence the behaviors of military and Biblical leaders.

Styles have *struggles,* as we have learned. A real challenge for **D** and **I** type leaders is that they start strong, but tend to leave a lot undone as they start something new. They are not usually strong finishers by nature. **S** and **C** type leaders may be hesitant to begin, but they usually stick with it and get the job done. Sometimes they have difficulty finishing on time, however, because they can keep fixing or improving until the deadline has passed.

We all struggle, but real leaders, of all styles, actually *pick themselves* to lead. By moving past their *natural* style limits, they can adapt and adjust to provide the vision and direction that those who are following need from their leader.

By this, I mean that some people, who typically would have stepped *back* into the shadows, have instead stepped out to show the way. Those who normally would have moved to the front of the line have instead gone to the back and picked up stragglers. They have "led from the rear." Some have spoken up when it would have been easier to keep quiet. Others have been quiet when their style is to speak out.

Currently, I am using a flying kite as my team leadership example in seminars. A number of factors must work together if the kite is going to take flight, and no single influence can take credit for the success of the team.

- The kite's strong frame is made for flight and takes all of the strain and stress in stride. It challenges the gravity that pulls it down. This reminds me of a **D**.
- The kite's colorful covering attracts attention but it's

real function is to create uplift. Without any reference to being full of air, it reminds me of the colorful, uplifting *I*.

- The string is unseen by most observers, but it provides resistance to the wind and keeps the kite anchored so it can soar, like an **S**.
- The tail is designed to maintain balance in flight. Its contribution may be evident, or it could occur internally, but **C**-like balance is always necessary.

When Henry Ford was asked who should be the leader in an organization, he replied that the question was like asking who should sing tenor in a quartet. "Obviously," he said, "it's the one who can do the job!" Personal style is never the main qualifying or limiting factor in leadership, but *character* often is!

In spite of their style and potential, our culture has seen many talented and gifted people who never became the great leaders they could have been. The failure of some wannabe leaders is that they are missing the authentic, *servant-heart* found in real leaders. While we temporarily may find a wannabe's *charisma* more attractive than a leader's *substance*, when the wannabe's followers tire of being manipulated, he'll find them missing too.

Just play the game

What if that study we mentioned earlier on job success and people skills *is* still true today? In my opinion, there can be no change in *business* that would make it untrue or irrelevant. Rather, there would have to be a fundamental change in *people* to alter its validity.

This may not be good news for you, if your *task* priority is such that you think business would improve if customers and employees would just stop showing up! (I know, some readers are wondering when I'm going to unload on all of the *people-oriented* individuals who are friendly but can't get anything done. That's the focus of *another* book. This one is on *relationships,* so it emphasizes the importance of *people* skills.) I acknowledge that *task-oriented* people have been very patient in reading thus far, and I want to sympathize with you that relationships are difficult. They are fluid and shift all the time. You desire a firmer foundation on which to build.

Still, as near as I can tell, this is the way the relationships game is played. If you don't like the rules, you can take it up with the Divine Designer, but I don't think He'll change them.

Or you can sit out life's game in protest of its rules, but that's not a good idea either. While you're protesting, others will be playing in your slot...and winning! The rules aren't all that hard and, once you get them down, you'll be able to understand and follow them more consistently to win. You'll also know when others have broken them. You'll know what plays to call to get your team back in the game. Eventually, you may even become so skilled that you become a world champion player. I hope you get to coach some other major league players too.

Having a *people-oriented* style doesn't make anyone

"people-smart," so there's no built-in advantage to those who suspect it might be otherwise. While some with *task-oriented* styles struggle to loosen up their people skills, many *people-oriented* individuals struggle to confine their style to more appropriate expressions.

Handling people well is an art, not a science. You evaluate and readjust. Sometimes you get it right and sometimes you reevaluate and readjust. You get better at relationships by practicing and correcting. Neither this book, nor others on the same theme, provide *pat answers*. Rather, their purpose is to provide *tools* you can use to be more effective.

From now on, as you read books on motivation, argumentation, negotiation, and presentation, remember to view them through the grid of your **DISC** insights. I'm not trying to discredit anything else you read about business or relationships. You will have to judge whether it's worthy to be applied in your life, just as you must with this information. Instead, I'm suggesting that you add to your *business* knowledge the knowledge, observations, and experience with personal styles that you have gained through this book.

There are many expert ideas and techniques pertaining to specific business situations, and entire volumes have been written about them. I'm not suggesting that my experience in the **DISC** language qualifies me to address the variety of suggestions and methods you'll find in those books. Ultimately, it's your life, your success, and your relationships that are involved, so it's your evaluation and your choice that determine what information has value for you.

Every *professional* interaction you experience involves

an element of *relationship*. We have focused on some of the relationship issues that can help, or hinder, your efforts to succeed professionally.

Because this has been a long section, and we've covered a lot of territory, here are the high points for review:

- Business is *people*-centered, not *product*-centered.
- Servicing *people's* needs is the basis for business success.
- Everyone is your customer: buyers, suppliers, employees, managers, and coworkers.
- Sometimes only someone else can meet your need, and people skills are your only tool to enlist their help.
- Meeting customer needs requires understanding the need and the customer.
- People do business with people they like, or with those who are like them.
- Negotiating is a people skill that all styles can learn, and each style has pieces of the puzzle.
- Negotiators can create a comfortable climate that leads to a win–win rather than a win–lose.
- Accountability is a key to business leadership.
- Personal Style Assessments can be beneficial in benchmarking, preemployment interviewing, performance review, and team-building.
- Leadership is more about character than style.
- Leadership requires skills and strengths from each style.

Chapter 24: Becoming People Smart

When my style's *strengths* are working for me, I am so very glad I have them. When my style's *struggles* are working against me, I wish I had a different style. My success, however, does not lie in changing my style, but in mastering it.

For a long time, I didn't understand my "wiring," so I made excuses for myself. Now, my understanding of **DISC** has given me tools that can move me from excuses to excellence. What will demonstrate its worthiness is how I live out every day according to what I have written in this book. After all, *books* have editors who take out the mistakes before everyone is invited to look. *Lives* are viewed as they occur.

The last chapters have been lengthy because they have involved broader applications of the basic information. This closing chapter will be short. Its purpose is to answer, "So what do I do now? Where do I go from here? What's my next step?"

Over my years of writing books and creating and presenting seminars, I've learned there is never enough time or space to convey every important idea. *Getting to Know You* is a general-interest book designed for readers who want an overall view of people skills and personal styles.

Of course, there is always more to learn. Here are some suggestions to make this information more personal and practical for you.

Bookmark us

First, I hope you'll bookmark *www.ChrisCarey.com* in your web browser. We attempt to address readers' questions and ideas through a **DISC** section. We offer a growing list of documents and articles that address specific needs, all downloadable to your computer. Our web site also provides access to books, books-on-tape, and other helpful products and resources.

Complete an assessment

Then, I hope you'll complete a Personal Style Assessment. A full-scale report is available through *www.ChrisCarey.com*. It's important to get to know yourself as well as you can through an accurate and reliable 4-factor instrument.

The on-line assessment we use has been validated in double-blind studies and used by several million people. In more than 20 pages, our in-depth report covers:
- General characteristics of your **D**, **I**, **S**, and **C** blend
- Your areas of *strength* and *struggle*
- Comparisons of your *natural* and *adapted* styles
- How you see yourself, and how others see you under stress
- Lists of *communication dos and don'ts*
- Your most productive work environment
- Team and organization contributions
- Motivation and management keys
- An action plan for personal improvement

Our assessment software creates specific reports for:
- Executives, managers and employees
- Sales skills
- Team-building
- Customer service
- Improving the work environment
- Career planning
- Time management
- Interviewing processes
- Communication skills
- Relationships for couples
- Parent/child rapport

The "survey" you filled out in this book is not the same as the validated assessment reports just described. The purpose of the survey was to give you some working knowledge of the **DISC** concept and to help you approximate your most intense and least intense traits. However, the full Personal Style Assessment Report provides insights that are closely matched to your responses. This is the report I mentioned that changed my life.

Share the information in the report with people in a position to assist you in reaching your life goals. Ask them to be an extra set of eyes and ears to compensate for your blind spots. They have already seen, in your behavior, the information on the report, but they will be glad to know that you see it now too. Doing this requires a little courage and humility on your part, they think—but the truth is that you are excited about your future! You're not going to be a "thermometer" anymore. You can be the "thermostat" and set the temperature rather than just observing it.

Read it again

My next recommendation is that you read this book again. It's too much to absorb in one reading, and this information will only add power to your relationships when you apply it intentionally, intelligently, and conscientiously.

Read more about personal styles

Next, I recommend that you read books specifically focused in your area of immediate interest. For instance:

- For help in personal styles and child-rearing issues: *Different Children, Different Needs* (Sisters, OR; Multnomah Press/Questar, 1994) by Charles F. Boyd, which uses **DISC** insights throughout.
- For adult relationship issues from a Biblical perspective: the **DISC**-based book, *Understanding How Others Misunderstand You* (Chicago, IL; Moody Press, 1995), by Ken Voges and Ron Braund.
- For cold-reading people's styles in a variety of settings and dealing with them accordingly: *The Art of Profiling: Reading People Right the First Time* (Richardson, TX; International Focus Press, 1997) by Dan Korem.
- For insights in business relationships: *The Platinum Rule: Discover the Four Basic Business Personalities and How They Can Lead You to Success* (New York, NY; Warner Books, 1998) by Anthony Alessandra, PhD and Michael J. O'Connor, PhD. It provides style-related tools for selling, managing, and practically everything else you need to do in business, with emphasis on "them" instead of "you."
- For insights into vocational education and career plan-

ning: *Your Career in Changing Times* (Chicago, IL; Moody Press, 1998) by Lee Ellis and Larry Burkett. There is also a companion workbook, *Finding the Career That Fits You* (Moody Press, 1998).

- For speaking to audiences with **DISC** in mind, read my book for entertainers, *Find the Stuff That's You: Discovering Who You Are and Letting the Audience In On It* (Pomeroy, OH; Lee Jacobs Productions, 2001).

Read more about your particular interests

There are numerous books that, while not **DISC**-oriented, have practical, people-smart insights that accommodate what you have learned about personal styles. My favorite business-oriented titles include:

- *The 21 Irrefutable Laws of Leadership: Follow Them and People Will Follow You* (Nashville, TN; Thomas Nelson Publishers, 1998) by John C. Maxwell. I saw **DISC**-related concepts on every page, and I hope John will write a book that makes the connection—or allow me to work on it with him!
- *Be A People Person: Effective Leadership Through Effective Relationships* (Colorado Springs, CO; Chariot Victor Books, 1994) by John C. Maxwell.
- *Becoming a Person of Influence* (Thomas Nelson Publishers, 1997) by John C. Maxwell and Jim Dornan.
- *Dynamic People Skills: Developing Relationships That Develop Success* (Wheaton, IL; Tyndale House Publishers, 1997) by Dexter Yager with Ron Ball.
- *Handling Diversity in the Workplace: Communication is the Key* (West Des Moines, IA; American Media Pub-

lishing, 1997) by Kay duPont, CSP.

- *Bringing Out the Best in People: How to Enjoy Helping Others Excel* (Minneapolis, MN; Augsburg Fortress Publishers, 1985) by Alan Loy McGinnis.

- *Compassionate Capitalism: People Helping People Help Themselves* (New York, NY; E.P. Dutton/Penguin Books, 1993) by Richard M. DeVos.

- *How to Win Friends and Influence People* (New York, NY; Pocket Books, 1994) by Dale Carnegie.

- *How I Raised Myself from Failure to Success in Selling* (New York, NY; Fireside/Prentice Hall, 1977) by Frank Bettger.

- *Reject Me—I Love It! 21 Secrets for Turning Rejection into Direction* (Hummelstown, PA; Success Publishers, 1997) by John Fuhrman.

- *Children Are Wet Cement* (Old Tappan, NJ; Fleming H. Revell Company, 1995) by Anne Ortlund.

Final words

The goal of this information has been to help you increase success in your personal and professional relationships. In all the words you've read, I hope the one that remains at the front of your memory is "appropriate." By responding to people and situations around you in more appropriate ways, you will increase your credibility and influence with others. You will solve your people puzzles!

What can you do next...?

As this information becomes helpful to you, please contact **ChrisCarey:CreativeCommunication, Inc.**, and let us know. Our web site offers a variety of services to assist you.

• To obtain your own *Personal Style Assessment Report*, you may complete a questionnaire—online, by e-mail, or by fax—that will produce our customized-to-you, 20+ page report detailing your personal style. It contains valuable insights for improving both professional and personal relationships.

• A free subscription to **Chris Carey's e-mail newsletter** is available on request.

• Additional **reference resources** are also available at our site.

Other products, available online and by mail, include:

 *The Price and The Prize* shows how you can get what you want and want it once you get it. This new book deals with change, goal-setting, management, and motivation for yourself and others.

Begin Again deals with how to start over, gain confidence, establish integrity, and build trust—especially after damage has occurred in personal relationships and professional reputations. A new book!

 *Solve Your "People Puzzles!"* is Chris Carey's 45-minute introductory DISC seminar on CD for use on your home computer. Chris's visuals and narration make it easy to understand.

Chris Carey presents **workshops, seminars, training,** and **keynote addresses** on subjects related to Solving Your People Puzzles™ for a wide variety of business groups, companies, organizations, associations, conferences, and conventions. For information on Chris Carey's products, consulting services, and speaking topics, please contact us through *www.ChrisCarey.com.*

About the Author

Chris Carey is a professional speaker, author, and consultant. In a variety of "live audience" venues, he has spoken to more than 5,000,000 people across North America, and in countries as far away as Saudi Arabia and Australia. He specializes in what he calls "people puzzles," helping businesses and individuals to:

- Understand their behavioral preferences
- Integrate their core values with actions
- Improve their communication skills
- Build more productive teams
- Lead and thrive in change
- Prioritize their life goals

Chris has written 6 books on entertainment production, communication skills, and personal style assessment and adjustment. He has ghostwritten and cowritten numerous books for speakers, trainers, and media celebrities, on topics such as investment risk, career guidance, classroom discipline, team-building, and multilevel marketing recruitment and retention.

His talents have served such organizations as McDonald's, Aramco, Six Flags, Sprint, LifePathways, Amway, Christian Financial Concepts, Thomas Nelson Company, Moody Press, Victory Over Violence, New South Wales Ministry of Education, and more. Chris has been honored by inclusion in the publications of *2000 Notable American Men, Outstanding Young Men in America, Who's Who Among Rising Young Americans,* and *International Who's Who of Professionals.* From 250,000 consultants worldwide, in the year 2000, he was one of only 10 honored as "Guru of the Year" by Guru, Inc., for exemplifying the "Guru lifestyle" in his business.

He is president of ChrisCarey:CreativeCommunication, Inc., in Atlanta, Georgia, and is most easily contacted through his corporate Internet address, *www.ChrisCarey.com.*

Endorsements

It pays to be people-smart! I am happy to recommend Getting to Know You *as a book that will enlarge your perspective and assist you in building relationships that go the distance. Whether you are just starting out on your own, or if you have a lifetime of experience, now is the right time to read this book!* — **Dr. John C. Maxwell**
founder of The INJOY Group
and author of *The 21 Irrefutible Laws of Leadership*

In Getting to Know You, *Chris Carey helped me to define and better understand the people I deal with. I thought I knew myself, but this helped me to understand others as well.* — **Rich DeVos**
Chairman and Owner, NBA Orlando Magic
Cofounder, Amway Corporation
and author of *Compassionate Capitalism*

Over many decades, I have found great success in demonstrating that "people are funny." Chris Carey also proves that "people are predictable!" The valuable, practical information he shares in Getting to Know You, *will help you find greater success in dealing with funny, predictable people. Read and grow as you enjoy his wonderful new book.*
— **Art Linkletter**
author of *Kids Say the Darndest Things*

Getting to Know You *is a fabulous book that will help you connect with anyone, anywhere—at home or at work. Buy it, read it, and you'll benefit from it greatly!* — **Tony Alessandra, PhD, CPAE, CSP**
author of *The Platinum Rule* and *Charisma*

Getting to Know You *provides a much-needed resource for understanding self and others. Chris Carey does a masterful job of presenting personality information that we can all relate to and use at work, home, and in every area of life.* — **Jerry Mabe**, President
Lee Ellis, Vice President
RightPath Resources, Inc.

Endorsements

One should emerge from the womb and immediately be presented with a copy of Getting to Know You. *Chris Carey's book is a blueprint for those who are ready to accept the challenge and adventure of creating more meaningful relationships in every aspect of their lives.*

— **Judy Suiter**
President, Competitive Edge, Inc.
Coauthor of *DISC: The Universal Language*

Chris Carey's new work, Getting to Know You, *is a real winner. He credits his predecessors in behavioral style research. He explains real-world interpersonal dynamics, and he addresses the gut-wrenching issues that make a difference today.* — **Don Hutson**
CEO, U. S. Learning, Inc.
Past President, National Speakers Association,
and author of *The Sale* and *The Contented Achiever*

Chris Carey has created a superb book that is a gold mine of information about people and why they do what they do. — **Roger Dawson**
author of *Secrets of Power Negotiating*

What a wonderful tool Chris has created! By simplifying how to understand both self and others, he has given all who read this great book the missing piece to their own life's puzzle. That piece fits very nicely in completing your own picture. — **John Furhman**
author of *Reject Me—I Love It:
21 Secrets for Turning Rejection into Direction*

This book is terrific! I have been recommending another book on this topic. From now on, I will recommend Getting to Know You *instead. It is well organized, very complete, and imminently practical. If you are going to buy only one book to help you understand and adapt to the behavior of others, this should be the one.* — **Mike Stewart, CSP**
author of *Close More Sales: Persuasion
Skills That Boost Your Selling Power*

Endorsements

Chris Carey put it all together! In his easy-to-read style, he offers valuable insights and practical help to improve every relationship in your life. Getting to Know You *is a must read for anyone who wants to succeed!*
— **Gene Swindell**
The Voice of Change™
President, Creative Concepts International, Inc.
and author of *The New ABCs of Success*

Chris Carey has written a book that I can easily recommend to all interested students who desire the factual, understandable explanations that are so easy to read.
- Who am I?
- How can I read and understand the behavior of strangers, friends, and loved ones?
- What knowledge will empower me and others to become more people relational?

The answers to these and related questions are answered in Getting to Know You—*a must read for individuals serious about achieving their God-given potential, professionally and personally.*
— **Ronald E. Strumbeck, EdD**
President, Potential Unlimited

I love this book—there are some important life lessons in it! For instance, Voltaire wrote, "All styles are good, except the tiresome sort," but Getting To Know You *helps us understand that there is room on the planet even for them—ya gotta get a copy to Voltaire!*
— **Roy Lantz**
President, Roy Lantz Seminars,
and author of *The Care and Keeping of Customers*

If you interact with other people (and who doesn't?), you need Chris Carey's new book, Getting to Know You. *He has taken the dry bones of personality typing and fleshed them out with real-life examples. Once I got the knack of it, adjusting my reactions to the personal styles I encountered became easy and effective. This book will make you a better communicator.*
— **Roger M. Scovil**
author of *Get Ahead: Scovil's 7 Rules for Success in Management*

Endorsements

I highly recommend this book. It is very informative, and it will quickly capture your attention. Getting to Know You will help you see yourself and others with a new perspective. — **Randal Ross**
author of *7 Habits of Winning Relationships*

I have met only a few writers who can explain complex issues in terms that everybody can understand. Chris Carey is one of those gifted authors. Without fail, I am able to teach more effectively because of his masterful translation of terms, buttressed by humorous, memorable illustrations. Getting to Know You is a book that will help readers understand that our goal is not to "change" people who seem different. Instead, we want to identify the traits that shape their profiles, and use that information to relate to these individuals more effectively. Equally significant, we will understand our own personal styles more clearly by reading this book. — **Bill Lampton, PhD**
President, Championship Communication
and author of *The Complete Communicator:
Change Your Communication, Change Your Life!*

Chris Carey has done a great job piecing together the personality puzzle in a way that is both understandable and practical. The insights he sets forth in this book will apply to every area of your life. — **Charles F. Boyd, DMin**
author of *Different Children, Different Needs*

Any serious student of communication will recognize that this is a rich mine of information. — **Gene Greissman, PhD**
author of *Time Tactics of Very Successful People*

Marketing is not just a question of understanding markets. It also involves understanding people. Chris Carey's new book will help everyone involved in a marketing program deal with the many different types of people that need to be reached. — **Al Ries**
Chairman, Ries & Ries, Marketing Strategists
coauthor of *The 22 Immutable Laws of Marketing:
Violate Them at Your Own Risk*

Endorsements

Once you understand yourself, you can then move to understanding what drives your behavior. Once you know, you can more easily make positive, lasting changes. Chris uses great illustrations and stories to hold your interest and make the learning memorable.

— **Chip Eichelberger**
President, Switched On! Keynotes and Seminars

Getting to Know You is a very useful book, both for business and personal relationships. It's easy to read and put into practice. I found it especially valuable as I was interviewing new employees and wanted to be sure to get the correct personality balance. I highly recommend this book to anyone hoping to better understand themselves, their colleagues, and their families. — **Snowden McFall**
President, Brightwork Advertising and Training,
and author of *Fired Up! How to Succeed by Making Your Dreams Come True*

Getting to Know You is a great book — a real "difference maker." Not only did it help me understand others better, I got to know myself better too! — **John Mason**
author of *An Enemy Called Average*

This book contains more practical ideas to help you be more effective with other people than anything else you will ever read. Outstanding!
— **Brian Tracy**
President, Brian Tracy International
author of *Maximum Achievement*

Chris Carey, in a delightful, illustrative, and often humorous manner, has helped to identify some of the personality traits that make up who we are and those with whom we are associated. For those who are interested in developing their people skills, this is a good read.

— **Dr. Robert H. Schuller**
The Crystal Cathedral
author of My Journey